CW00819318

SMART

TO

WISE

MIKE CLAYTON

Marshall Cavendish
Business

Copyright © 2012 Mike Clayton
Cover art by Cover Kitchen

Published in 2012 by Marshall Cavendish Business
An imprint of Marshall Cavendish International

PO Box 65829
London EC1P 1NY, United Kingdom
info@marshallcavendish.co.uk
and
1 New Industrial Road, Singapore 536196
genrefsales@marshallcavendish.com
www.marshallcavendish.com/genref

Other Marshall Cavendish offices: Marshall Cavendish International (Asia) Private Limited,
1 New Industrial Road, Singapore 536196 • Marshall Cavendish Corporation, 99 White Plains
Road, Tarrytown, NY 10591 • Marshall Cavendish International (Thailand) Co Ltd. 253 Asoke,
12th Flr, Sukhumvit 21 Road, Klongtoey Nua, Wattana, Bangkok 10110, Thailand • Marshall
Cavendish (Malaysia) Sdn Bhd, Times Subang, Lot 46, Subang Hi-Tech Industrial Park, Batu
Tiga, 40000 Shah Alam, Selangor Darul Ehsan, Malaysia

Marshall Cavendish is a trademark of Times Publishing Limited

A CIP record for this book is available from the British Library

ISBN 978 981 4361 42 2

Printed and bound by CPI Group (UK) Ltd, Croydon, CR0 4YY

TABLE OF CONTENTS

To Sophia, goddess of wisdom,

and my own smart, wise child;

the indirect inspiration for this book.

ACKNOWLEDGEMENTS

Four people had a direct hand in the genesis of this book: Sophia Clayton, Felicity Clayton, Paula Gardner and Martin Liu, my publisher.

But there have been many wise people who have influenced this book over the years, none more than my father. How can I name them all? And how can I ever be sure that I have not left someone out? Safest then to be selective and name only the strongest influences: Roger French, David Dixon, Emma Francis, Professor Henry Hall, George Owen, John Everett...

How can I write a book about wisdom without acknowledging all of the truly great and wise thinkers and authors, whose work has influenced and shaped me? They occupy the shelves of the libraries of any civilised nation – until they are removed for use, and truly come alive. To all of them, thank you. And thank you too, to the BBC, for much of your output over the years, and especially for Radio 4!

Introduction:
WISDOM

You're smart. You know stuff. You've made great strides in your career and your life. But you know there's more: there are levels that you aren't ready for yet. There are things you want to do and people you want to impress that you can't yet reach. Because being smart is not enough. Being smart will only get you so far – to achieve all that you can, people need to see you as more than smart. They need to see you as wise.

> *"Wisdom is a rare commodity. There are a lot of very brilliant people, bright people, clever people; not so many people who are wise."*
>
> **Malcolm Fraser, Prime Minister of Australia from 1975 to 1983**

WHAT IS WISDOM?

Each dictionary has its own definition of wisdom. Some are very long; others are commendably short. They talk about the ability to think, to know what is true or right, to apply knowledge and be sensible. They talk about shrewdness, erudition and enlightenment. Let's start with something simple.

> *wisdom: "ability to use your knowledge well"*

As you read this book, you will see how many different interpretations there are. We'll take ideas from ancient Chinese, Indian and Greek traditions, and from modern philosophy, psychology and social science.

Indeed, the ancient Greeks had two different words that we translate as "wisdom". These give us the two main aspects of wisdom:

Theoretical Wisdom

"Sophia" is the wisdom we have about our world and its phenomena. It is about using our knowledge and reason to search for truth and gain deep insights into reality.

Practical Wisdom

"Phronesis" is the wisdom we show when we have understood reality and make choices that change our world for the better.

The Humility of Wisdom

A Greek legend has it that the Oracle at Delphi declared the philosopher Socrates to be the wisest of all the Greeks. Socrates reasoned that this was because he alone knew that he did not know anything. A wise person must, first of all, be humbled by the vast wealth and variety of knowledge and experiences that are available to us all, and know the limits of their own comprehension.

FROM SMART TO WISE

Smart to Wise is about how to become wise. It does not set out to give you the answers or to dispense wisdom, but to show you the direction of your journey. There are many routes – and many possible destinations. *Smart to Wise* offers you a list of some of the places to visit along the way and some of the souvenirs to collect, which will mark your progress to your own place of wisdom. Where that is, and how you will get there, is for you to discover.

Where are you going?

How will you get there?

Where are you starting from?

These are not glib questions. Although perfect answers are not possible; wisdom demands that you engage with questions like these and start to form your response. From here on, you need to be prepared to spend time thinking about important matters.

"Smart" or "Wise"?

Let's draw a distinction between "smart" and "wise". If you are smart, you will know how things work – how to get on. Smart is a matter of learning the rules and being able to follow them. Wisdom needs more. How will you cope when the rules don't apply? How will you manage in a new environment where you don't know the rules? What rules would you work to when there are none?

Wisdom requires experience to understand the real world as it is, in all of its complexity, rather than the narrow context in which you grew smart. Can you accurately interpret the new events, patterns and behaviours to discern what's really going on, and determine what needs to be done? If you can, that's wisdom.

Smart is necessary but it isn't sufficient if you want to reach your full potential, and play a leading role in your family, work and society.

SEVEN PILLARS OF WISDOM

> *"Wisdom has built her home; she has hewn her seven pillars."*
>
> **Proverbs 9:1**

<small>FIGURE 1. SEVEN PILLARS OF WISDOM</small>

The Old Testament alludes to wisdom as offering herself to any who will come, and promising great rewards to those who seek her out:

> *"In my hands are riches and honour, boundless wealth and the rewards of virtue. My harvest is better than gold."*

The Bible uses the number seven to indicate a complete set. When we seek out what marks wisdom and the transition from smart to wise, we readily find seven pillars.

First Pillar	Self-Mastery
Second Pillar	Perception
Third Pillar	Evolution
Fourth Pillar	Conduct
Fifth Pillar	Judgement
Sixth Pillar	Fairness
Seventh Pillar	Authority

These pillars can be arranged in two tiers, with numbers 1 to 4 forming the basis for wisdom, and numbers 5 to 7 forming the final support. The journey from smart to wise will require you to build each of these pillars strongly, and set them upon a firm foundation.

First Pillar:
SELF-MASTERY

WISDOM AS SELF-AWARENESS

> *"Let it be your constant method to look into the design*
> *of people's actions, and see what they would be at, as*
> *often as it is practicable; and to make this custom the*
> *more significant, practice it first upon yourself."*
>
> **Marcus Aurelius**

Many of the qualities we value most in people can only be gained when they have high levels of self-awareness. Poise, dignity, composure, and even gravitas come from knowing and being comfortable with who you are. We turn to people with these traits in times of need.

What we interpret as composure is a calmness that comes from inner strength and an ability to cope with the most challenging situations. We see poise and dignity when people can detach themselves from a situation sufficiently to see things objectively, putting fear and anxiety aside. The solidity of character that we call gravitas depends on a firm grasp of who you are and a steadfast commitment to integrity.

KNOW YOURSELF

The start of your journey from smart to wise is discovering who you really are. The following questions are ones you will want to come back to again and again…

Sixteen Questions for Your Journey

- Where do I come from?
- Where am I going?
- What motivates me?
- What do I fear?
- What is important to me?
- What do I want?
- What will I stand and fight for? … and what will I stand and fight against?
- What am I grateful for?
- What work will bring me joy?
- How will I measure my life?
- What am I living for?
- Who has had a major influence on me?
- Whom do I cherish?
- Whom do I fear?
- Whom do I serve?
- Who am I?

Start a notebook or journal, as you might for any journey. In it write these sixteen questions; and any others that are important to you. From time to time, sit down quietly and think about these questions. Write your thoughts in your journal.

If you have started to think about these questions, then you will have surveyed only half of who you are: the half that is already known to you. What about the part of you that is currently unknown to you?

How do Other People Perceive You?

You may not be fully conscious of the way you come across to the world. People around us often recognise traits, habits or characteristics to which we ourselves are oblivious. These may be strengths or failings.

Your "Dark Side"

Jung described the *"shadow aspect"* as the part of your unconscious mind that holds strengths and weaknesses you are unaware of and, more importantly, that you want to hide from the world. It is responsible for many of your instincts.

> *"Everyone carries a shadow and the less it is embodied in the individual's conscious life, the blacker and denser it is."*
>
> **Carl Jung**

Self-mastery involves acknowledging this part of who you are, and learning from it.

Seek Feedback

The more that you can learn about yourself, and the more sources that you can tap into, the better. Here are some ideas:

1. Take a friend or colleague out for lunch and ask them questions. Listen carefully without trying to respond.
2. Ask one or two of your staff to "give it to you straight". If you don't hear any meaningful criticisms, suspect that there is a fear factor. This is valuable information.
3. Find out if your human resources (HR) team at work can arrange for 360-degree feedback in which bosses, peers and subordinates offer anonymous assessments and commentary.
4. Invest in psychometric testing using tools such as the Myers-Briggs Type Indicator (MBTI), the 16 Personality Factors (16PF), the DISC psychometric test (Dominance, Influence, Steadiness and Compliance), the Strength Deployment Inventory (SDI) or the VIA Signature Strengths survey (for Values in Action).
5. Find a mentor who can assess your performance from the perspective of greater experience. This may be someone from your workplace, a professional membership body, a social grouping or from your wider circle of contacts.
6. Look out for personal development workshops that can give you insights into yourself from new perspectives.
7. If you are struggling with a particular issue, consider seeking coaching or counselling from a suitably trained professional.
8. Try the Johari Window exercise on the following page.

To make the most of what you learn, consider seeking support from an experienced coach to help you understand and process what you learn.

The Johari Window

Developed by and named after Joseph Luft and Harry Ingram, the Johari Window sets out four areas of our lives, as illustrated in Figure 2. The window has four panes, representing the knowledge or lack of it that we have about ourselves, and that others have about us.

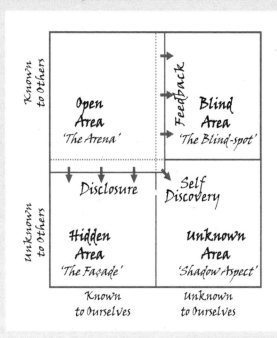

FIGURE 2: THE JOHARI WINDOW

The Arena

The Open area contains what we and the people around us all know about ourselves. Because we share this knowledge, it is the basis of effective communication. Luft and Ingham suggested that the more of our life that is in this quadrant, the better our relationships will be.

You can discover your open area by selecting five or six adjectives that best describe you from a list of 56 they developed. Then ask others to select which ones they think describe you. The adjectives that match represent your arena.

The Façade
In the Hidden area is the information about yourself that you have not revealed to others. It may be trivial facts about hobbies, deeply personal feelings, or past history that you are embarrassed or secretive about. You extend your open area by disclosing some of your façade.

The Blind Spot
In the Blind area, people around you can recognise traits, habits or characteristics, to which you are oblivious. These may be strengths or failings. You can extend your open area by securing feedback from others about how they perceive you – the things that they notice but don't normally mention about your behaviours, style, and habits.

The Shadow Aspect
Finally, there is the Unknown area, representing characteristics that neither we nor other people are aware of. Perhaps these things are repressed; perhaps simply un-expressed, like latent capabilities. This is what Jung described as your shadow aspect. It requires a journey of self-discovery to uncover these things.

The 56 Adjectives

able - accepting - adaptable - bold - brave - calm - caring - cheerful - clever - complex - confident - dependable - dignified - energetic - extroverted - friendly - giving - happy - helpful - idealistic - independent - ingenious - intelligent - introverted - kind - knowledgeable - logical - loving - mature - modest - nervous - observant - organised - patient - powerful - proud - quiet - reflective - relaxed - religious - responsive - searching - self-assertive - self-conscious - sensible - sentimental - shy - silly - smart - spontaneous - sympathetic - tense - trustworthy - warm - wise - witty

Who you are is complex. It is moulded by your experiences, and affects the impact you have on the world and people around you.

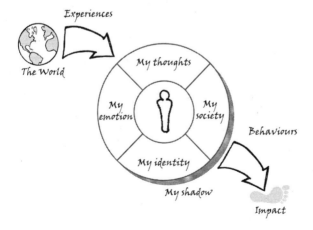

FIGURE 3: THE WHOLE YOU

BE YOURSELF

"This above all: to thine own self be true."
William Shakespeare, *Hamlet*: Act 1, Scene 3

What Shakespeare means by this is that we should do only what is "authentic" to our own natures: we must act with integrity. When you are not true to yourself and do not act according to your conscience, this represents what Socrates referred to as a *"corruption of the soul"* which, he argues, is the greatest of all evils.

This is a very modern theme. Philosophers from Kierkegaard to Heidegger to Sartre and Camus all discussed *"authenticity"*. In their terms, authenticity is about more than simply being true to yourself: it is about being true to the situation, as you perceive it. This contrasts with blindly following general rules or conventions. Wisdom is about choosing to act in a way that meets the needs of the situation quite precisely, and recognising when its complexity renders simple rules inappropriate.

When you can do this, you will start to create the balance of confidence and humility that characterises wisdom: confidence in who you are and in your choices, yet humble enough to know that each choice may be compromised by your own limitations.

Accept Your Limitations

The self-help movement and many motivational speakers will tell you that you can do anything and be anything that you choose. Your limitations are simply those that you choose to accept.

"Argue for your limitations, and sure enough, they're yours."

Richard Bach, *Illusions*

This is a phenomenally motivating quotation, and is very popular in self-help circles. It means that you can achieve much more than you might think possible, if you challenge the faulty thinking and limiting beliefs that constrain what you are willing to aim for and tackle. With the right resources, knowledge and determination, you can reach much that lies over your horizon.

But this is not to say that you do not have limitations. In particular, there are limits to your current knowledge. Wisdom requires you learn to recognise and accept these limits, and to distinguish conclusions that you draw from within your domains of experience, expertise and skill, from those that do not. To paraphrase the philosopher Ludwig Wittgenstein: "If you have nothing useful to say about it, shut up."

Seek Out Work that Brings You Joy

People who, by consensus, are thought to be wise tend to have one thing in common: work is important to all of them, and they all do work that they enjoy. Find a career or a role that gives you satisfaction, and allows you to experiment, to take risks and to learn. Figure 4 may help you to find out what that task is.

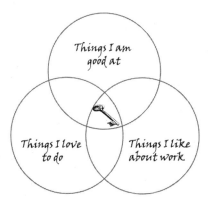

FIGURE 4: WHERE TO FIND WORK THAT BRINGS YOU JOY

Where is Your Joy?

Think about the choices you have made – big ones or small ones – that have brought you pleasure, satisfaction, fulfilment or even joy.

- What has driven those choices?
- What aspects of the outcome have brought you joy?
- How would you have felt if those choices had led you to different outcomes?
- Was the choice or the outcome more important to you?

These principles will lead you to your real values in life. They may be about achievement, harmonious relationships, power and control, fun and laughter, learning, influence and status, or your own form of spirituality. How can you find a work role that aligns closely with your values?

BUILD INNER STRENGTH

Many cultures revere courage as an important virtue: but what is courage? It is not an absence of fear but rather, the ability to overcome your fear and act anyway. Courage is an inner strength and the word comes from the same root as the French word "cœur": heart. The ability to bravely face whatever comes at you demands an ability to cope in any situation.

Smart people get by in times of adversity. The wise ones are those who can discern the right things to do, which will protect what they most value. They may rise conspicuously, as "winners", because their focus is not on the short-term and the next opportunity; but unlike the merely smart, their inspiration will help others to survive and thrive.

Resilience

Whether you face uncertainty or change, obstacles or setbacks, confusion or pain, your ability to do more than just cope, and yet remain true to who you are, is a measure of your wisdom. Perhaps one of the profoundest pieces of wisdom is the proverb *"this too shall pass"*. It means that all setbacks and all gains are transitory.

Martin Seligman, Lyn Abramson and John Teasdale discovered this as one of the foundations of psychological resilience: our ability to deal with adversity. They identified three styles of thought that mark out the distinction between those who give up and those who persevere. These are the ways in which we explain to ourselves – mostly unconsciously – what has happened.

"Permanence"

Optimists see bad events as temporary; pessimists see them as part of a permanent pattern. The authors describe the "this too shall pass" attitude to misfortune in terms of permanence.

"Pervasiveness"

Pessimists see setbacks as arising from a universally adverse situation while optimists see them as arising from specific circumstances.

"Personalisation"

Pessimists see adversity as arising from their faults, yet success as due to an outside agency such as "luck"; while optimists take responsibility for their contribution to successes and correctly assess the role of external agencies in their failures.

We will come back to pervasiveness and personalisation when discussing the role of perception in moving from smart to wise.

Gratitude

Fortunately for most of us, life is not all adversity. Yet some people go through life forever wanting more. Smart is about looking for the next opportunity, while wise is about building and growing. Foolishness is to never find fulfilment or contentedness with what you have – no matter what your achievements. The solution to balancing a vital concern for growth with a healthy contentment is *"gratitude"*. The wise are able to be grateful for what they have as well as make an honest assessment of what they still want.

Gratitude Journal

Create a *"gratitude journal"*. Take a notebook and, at least once a day, note down one thing for which you feel grateful at that time. It may be a big part of your life that you have been aware of today, or a small event during the day. Feel free to record more than one thing.

To hasten your move from smart to wise, take another few minutes to write a short commentary when you have written your gratitude: what can you learn from what you have just written? This process can enhance your sense of well-being in good times and provide a powerful way to support you when life is at its toughest.

The Wisdom of the Tao

Taoism is an ancient Chinese philosophical system that emphasises awareness and acceptance of the flow of nature. In Taoism, everything is as it should be, without absolving us from our obligation to make things better tomorrow. Taoism embodies many contradictions: non-action ("wu wei") is a key principle, for example, but Taoism also reminds us that getting things done is an essential part of life.

Lao Tzu said, "wu wei er wu bu wei" – *"No action, yet nothing is not done"*.

CULTIVATE DETACHMENT

"Looking at life's situations from a distance is the first step toward finding a solution and preventing them from happening again. By separating yourself from your experiences, you are able to move on with your life. If you don't, you're stuck in the puddle of the past without a paddle."

Wally "Famous" Amos

Many religious systems place a premium on detachment – the ability to separate yourself from material desires and the pressures of the everyday world. This starts to create a sense of contentment.

If you want to see the world clearly for what it is, and to understand the concerns of the people around you, you also need to be able to avoid your emotions becoming entangled with your perceptions. This is what psychologists refer to as *emotional detachment:* a form of mental discipline for creating boundaries. These boundaries can:

- Protect you from being hurt by other people's need to be dependent upon you
- Let other people be themselves, rather than what you want them to be
- Allow you to be free of a self-imposed responsibility for others' welfare

- Help you to avoid being manipulated by other people's controlling behaviours

Compassionate Detachment

Sometimes you will want to help someone or change something. Emotional detachment is not about becoming uncaring or unconcerned with others, but rather the ability to step out of the emotional realm when you choose to, so that you can see more clearly what is happening, and how best to respond.

You may also choose to not intervene. Letting go, so that people can be themselves, and make their own choices; and restraining your impulse to help them, rescue them or even "fix" them is not the same as "not caring". Accepting that you cannot control or change someone without their permission – or even that you know what is best for them – is, perhaps, the greatest respect you can pay them.

Detaching Yourself from Unhealthy Entanglements

Unhealthy entanglements are emotional ties to people, places, status or other things that do not serve you well. An over-dependency may be holding you back from learning and growing, or it could simply prevent you from reading situations objectively, thus clouding your judgement and introducing faulty thinking.

Step 1: List your emotional ties and evaluate each one.
- Which serve you by, for example, giving you pleasure, challenging your thinking, providing necessary resources?
- And which drain you by tapping energy, constraining your options, or seizing your focus?

- Where do you have an over-dependency?

Step 2: Let go of your beliefs that you need these attachments, that you can change or fix their objects, or that you have any absolute dependence upon them. You can do this when you:
- Identify the sources of harm arising from these attachments
- Examine what irrational beliefs are driving your unhealthy emotions
- Take control over your feelings and give yourself permission to let go of the old emotions

Step 3: Accept that there are some things outside of yourself that you cannot change, and that you have no responsibility for changing. You do not need to feel guilt or remorse for making this choice. Affirm your right to make your own choices and to take responsibility for them.

Step 4: If you need to, seek out support and help in the form of guidance, counselling or simply someone to talk to.

Step 5: Continue to choose your emotional attachments carefully.

Freedom from Fear

Only by separating your emotions from a situation can you escape the sensation of fear. This is important in acquiring wisdom, because failure along the way is inevitable. Fear of failure will stop you from doing what is right. One of the agents of fear is that little voice in your head. Helpful self-talk will draw your attention to what can go wrong and its consequences, but it becomes toxic when that is all that you can focus on.

You must learn to control this voice and listen instead to an analysis of the resources you have, to evade risks and counter errors. You must tell yourself where you can reasonably control the situation and reinforce your self-confidence and motivation. You must let this voice acknowledge – and even praise – your successes.

Failure should not be something that you fear, because you will learn far more from it than you will from your successes.

Merging the Traditions

Ancient Chinese philosophy had much to say about the nature of wisdom.

The oldest tradition is Taoism. Chuang Tzu wanted us to free ourselves from a compulsion to respect convention so that we can see clearly ("ming") and act spontaneously ("wu wei") and authentically. We will come back to the topic of clear perception in the next chapter. Over 600 years later, in his commentary on Chuang Tzu's work, Kuo Hsiang emphasised that wisdom is a matter of character; not knowledge.

The Confucian tradition emerged in the sixth century BCE at the same time as Lao Tzu was first writing about Taoism, in the Tao Te Ching. The interpreters of Confucius saw wisdom in a different light, as something that could be achieved through investigation. In the twelfth century, Zhu

Xi advocated mastering your mind and controlling your emotions through studying books, conversing with wise individuals or engaging in public services. Two hundred and fifty years later, Wang Yang-Ming put his emphasis on reflection, contemplation and meditation – almost a Buddhist approach.

Can we reconcile these great thinkers? We can. Wisdom comes from the ability to synthesise conflicting ideas and take from them the truths they hold to form a new, more complete truth.

Second Pillar:
PERCEPTION

WISDOM AS INTUITION

You are hoping to reach a point in your career, a place in your society or a status among your community where people seek out your opinions for your wisdom: your ability to spot opportunities or identify problems from the sparsest indications. The skill at the heart of this is intuition. In the earlier stages of your career, wisdom will set you above your peers, letting you evaluate a situation accurately and determine the correct response. This practical wisdom also requires intuition.

Intuition is formed from a cluster of skills called "perception" and "judgement". These will be vital in your journey from smart to wise, and intuition ties them together. When you understand how intuition works, you can also recognise the ways in which it can fail you.

PERCEIVE CLEARLY

How well do you really use your senses? When you look, what do you truly see; when you listen, how much do you hear, what details do you feel when you touch; what flavours can you taste when you eat; and how deeply do you smell when you inhale?

Many of us take our senses for granted and use only the tiny fraction of our perception that we need to navigate through life, for our duties and for our social relationships. Wisdom requires you to see, hear, feel, taste and smell more deeply than those around you; to become attuned to the reality beneath the surface.

The first step is never to be satisfied with your first impression. There will certainly be a truth in what you perceive, but when you go deeper, there will be more that you have yet to uncover.

The second step is to cultivate an ability to shift your focus from the global to the microscopic. We tend to focus at "the human level" and see things on our own scale. Or, we become seduced by the scale that is presented to us. Always challenge the bias of scale and pan out for the "big picture" or zoom in to the detail. It is not so much about "seeing the wood for the trees" as being able to choose to see the global ecosystem the wood sits within, the long-term history and future of the wood, as well as the range of species of trees, plants, animals, insects, fungi and micro-organisms, all the way down to the details of those micro-organisms.

Developing your Perception through Attention

The Buddha's Noble Eightfold Path starts with "right understanding", which means to perceive reality as it is, not as it appears to be. Many of the meditative disciplines of Buddhism are designed to help to develop this perception. You can also develop your perception in other ways.

Focused Attention: Seeing

Go to your local art gallery and pick a work of art that you do not know well. Study it intensely for ten minutes. See each detail and how it relates to the whole. How does the artist use colour? What are the effects they create? What are the shapes and patterns? What does the image convey to you? What mood and emotions does it conjure up?

Repeat this exercise from time-to-time; with art, magazine images, views of landscapes, in rooms and with faces. Practice seeing the things most people will miss.

Focused Attention: Hearing

Sit with your eyes closed and listen to the sounds you can hear. Pick out individual noises and listen intently. Where exactly do they come from? What movement do they convey? What is causing each sound and, with human sounds, what emotions and meaning do they carry? What can you predict from what you are hearing?

Another way to practice your listening is to put on headphones and listen to music. Give it your total attention. Listen to music that is unfamiliar and listen to familiar music for detail you've missed. Try classical music for this exercise; jazz also works well.

In the classical repertoire, try one of this magnificent ten: Bach's Brandenburg concertos, Beethoven's Symphonies Nos. 5 and 9, Brahms' Symphony No. 4, Haydn's Symphony No. 104, Mozart's Jupiter Symphony and his Requiem, Strauss's Thus Spake Zarathustra, Stravinsky's Rite of Spring and Vivaldi's Four Seasons.

Focused Attention: Smell and Taste

Smell and taste are intimately connected and often what we think we taste is actually a smell that is reaching our olfactory organs via the back of our mouth. Try it out: ask someone to blindfold you and offer various items for you to sniff. Practice describing what you smell. As you get better attuned, practice on more subtle differences such as varieties of apple or different wines. To test your taste on its own, ask someone to blindfold you and apply a nose clip. You may be surprised at how bland some of the things that you assumed taste strongly are. Take off the nose clip and try again to learn the difference.

Try taste tests of different varieties or qualities of the same product, like cheeses, apples, coffee or chocolate. Articulate in words the differences in smell, taste, colour, texture and all of the qualities that you can observe.

Defocused Attention

One of the paradoxes of perception is that we can absorb more information when we do not focus on any single part of it. Focus robs us of much of our ability to perceive things outside the narrow zone of focus. Defocussing allows us perception over a broader domain and to seize information more equally from each region.

Try allowing your eye muscles to relax and let your vision go out of focus. One way to do this is to imagine a dot straight ahead, at eye-level, in the far distance, and concentrate on that. Now allow your hearing to relax in the same way.

You will be pleasantly surprised by how much detail you can pick up and by how quickly you can return your focus to a particularly salient detail. You will see more than usual, hear more than usual, and have a greater sense of connection to your environment. This makes a very effective way to attend a presentation or meeting, and a good way to scan a crowd for a missing person, or a room for misplaced keys.

Modes of Perception

There are five ways of perceiving the world around you. Let's examine the merits of each.

Empirical

This is the gold standard of perception, which allows only objective observation of the real world to provide input into your interpretation of the world.

> "Take nothing on its looks: take everything on the evidence. There is no better rule."
>
> **Charles Dickens, *Great Expectations***

This is truly difficult because our senses can let you down. Indeed, generations of Western Philosophers from Descartes on have debated whether we can know of the existence of an external world with any certainty – and the debate continues. Kant was scandalised that nobody had been able to prove that it even exists. Perhaps a more fruitful approach, championed by Heidegger, is to set your concerns about reality aside and behave as if it does.

Focus on the evidence of your senses and spend the time honing your perception and looking for ever stronger empirical evidence.

Rational

Rational perception starts with a basis of observation and builds from it with reason and analysis.

> *"It is my intention first to cite experience, then to demonstrate through reasoning why experience must operate in a given way."*
>
> **Leonardo da Vinci**

Psychological

A subjective perception based on reading body language, expression and emotional cues. This can be very accurate if you attune yourself to the signals and learn to interpret them accurately. This ability is called empathy and can, quite literally, give you insights into what another person is thinking and how they are feeling.

Mythological

Perceiving the use and meaning of symbols, metaphors and archetypes is a perilous exercise. Symbolism is often highly culturally determined and even deeply personal, so there is a high likelihood of misperception and inaccurate onward communication. A deep sensitivity to the cultural signs that pertain to your culture is a necessary part of wisdom.

Mystical

There is no place in wisdom for superstitious thinking that takes unlikely or unexplained events as anything other than the product of chance or the absence of sufficient information. This is lazy and leads to blind faith, trust in luck and susceptibility to fraudsters. It is perfectly reasonable to concede that there are some things that you do not know, but wholly irrational to attribute something to a cause that is neither verifiable nor falsifiable.

Skilled Listening

An ability to listen intensely is one of the traits most often associated with wisdom. We all value someone who can give us their total attention and make us feel that they understand our message absolutely and completely. The essential elements of first-class listening are:

1. Turn to completely face the person you are listening to and look them in the eye.
2. Ask open questions and give supportive responses.
3. Turn off your mind to all distractions, including that little voice in your head.
4. Notice everything; not just the words, but expressions, gestures, posture. Practice de-focused attention.
5. Refrain from making judgements about what you hear, or offering advice unless asked.
6. Allow them to finish before thinking about your response or next question.
7. Don't be afraid of silence – it can be your greatest ally.
8. Reflect what you hear using their words, rather than rephrase it with yours.

Skilled listening is one of the key tools for social awareness – the ability to read people and interpersonal situations. Most of the available tools and models simply codify and make accessible knowledge that is deeply embedded in the human instinct. This is true for everyone with normal social and emotional development and is noticeably absent in people with autistic spectrum disorders.

Building Social Awareness

There are tools and models available to help you to interpret social situations and individual behaviour, from simple personality diagnostics like the Myers Briggs Type Indicator (MBTI) or the Merrill Reid Social Styles, to guidance on reading body language, to psychological tools for analysing social interactions, such as Transactional Analysis (TA).

The Link Between Perception and Knowledge

The English word "wise" comes from a much older word that meant "to see".

Indo-European	*woid / *weid / *wid	"see"
Indo-European	*wittos (pp)	"seen"
Prehistoric Germanic	*witanan	"to have seen"
Prehistoric Germanic	*witjan	"knowledge"
Prehistoric Germanic	*wisaz	"knowing"
Old English	wis	"knowing"
English	Wise and hence wisdom	

The words *vision* and *video* (Latin for "I see") have the same origin, as does the name of the ruling council in Anglo Saxon times, the *witangemot*.

* An asterisk indicates an inferred word form, for which there is no written evidence.

INTERPRET MEANING

"This thing, what is it in itself, in its own constitution?
What is its substance and material? And what its
causal nature? And what is it doing in the world?"

Marcus Aurelius

Interpreting meaning requires rational thinking at its very best. Meaning implies either a logical or causal connection between two things. The mistake that we often make, however, is to assign meaning without sufficient evidence, through faulty or mystical thinking. Always ask: *"How do I know this? What is the evidence?"* In so doing, we are following Aristotle's principle of "saving the appearances". That is, we must reject any explanation that contradicts the evidence or goes beyond experience.

Cause and Effect

To move from smart to wise, you must acquire a clear understanding of cause and effect and, in particular, you need to be able to spot faulty arguments that wrongly allege causation. Indeed, in realms from politics to problem solving, an essential skill is the ability to discern not just cause, but root cause. Here, real wisdom eschews simple and unitary answers and recognises that there could be a great many causal conditions that contribute to a single event.

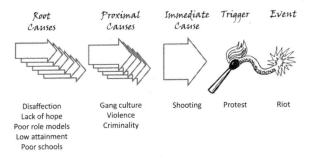

FIGURE 5: THE CHAIN OF CAUSE AND EFFECT

Figure 5 shows that events can have (and usually do have) a sequences of causes. The further back you go the more fundamental the factor, but even this illustration is gross simplification of how reality works. Make a decision to reject over-simplifications and embrace subtle analysis and the complexity of many inter-connected factors contributing to events.

Post hoc, ergo propter hoc
This Latin phrase translates as *"after this, therefore because of this"* and represents a common form of faulty interpretation of events. It is wrong to assume that just because B follows A, then A was the cause of B.

An example: I get a cold, so I take my granny's cold cure. I get better. Therefore I might conclude that the cold cure caused me to get well. Alternatively, I also know that colds do run their course and will resolve themselves after a few days, with no intervention.

Correlation does not equal causation

This statement corrects a common fallacy that you will hear and read again and again in news, legal, political and workplace contexts. Simply because two things happen together, it does not mean that there is a causal link between them. They may be wholly unconnected (coincidences do occur), or they may be both linked to a common cause or cluster of interlinked causes.

As an example, consider the statement: "wealthy people are better drivers". Wealthy drivers do indeed suffer fewer road traffic fatalities, so on the face of it, this is true. However, wealthy drivers tend to have bigger and better maintained cars. They also tend to be older and therefore less impulsive. Perhaps these are more instrumental in the fatality rate.

Spotting Trends

Tracking back from an event to its cause is relatively easy. What takes great wisdom is accurately tracking forward from a change, a situation or an event to spot the future effect. Understanding trends and interpreting them accurately will take all of your experience, intuition and wisdom.

The process by which a new product, technology or idea grows from a good idea to a global phenomenon is called *"diffusion"*. Spotting a trend means not just evaluating the idea at its core, but understanding the processes by which opinion leaders communicate the idea and others take it up. This means placing your ear to the societal conversations around you and having a strong cultural sensitivity to evaluate and interpret the details of these conversations correctly.

> *"Matters of small concern should be treated seriously."*
> **Yamamoto Tsunetomo,** *Hagakure*

The Sceptic Tradition

The Sceptics doubted everything. In this sense, they were intellectual descendants of Socrates, who lived a hundred years earlier (470–399 BCE). Philosophical scepticism was developed by Pyrrho (365–270 BCE), a soldier in Alexander the Great's army. Seeing the world, and valuing its diverse cultures, he realised that no one opinion should prevail – each culture had beliefs that were contradicted by another. So he rejected absolute knowledge, stating that it was unattainable; going further than Socrates who merely asserted that he did not have it.

Certainty is impossible, the Sceptics said, because any proof must depend upon one or more unproven premises – in mathematics, these are known as axioms. As Nietzsche was to say 2,200 years later:

"There are no facts, only interpretations."

The sceptics argued that the only evidence that we have is in how things appear, but that these appearances can deceive us. So never assume the truth of one explanation. Instead, examine all arguments to make the best assessment of the reality you face and act accordingly. This may not be true scepticism, but perhaps it is a form of practical scepticism.

DEVELOP INTUITION

Intuition is our ability to extract a small amount of essential data from a highly complex situation and make sense of it at a level beneath our conscious awareness. It is often the means by which we can spot a trend from what appear to be the tiniest of hints.

You will often have found that, when you make a decision that conflicts with your intuition, it turns out to be a poor one and sometimes, when you make a good decision that follows your intuition, you are unable to understand how you were so sure that the decision was right.

Intuition allows you to:
- Sense when something is wrong
- Draw rapid, accurate conclusions in a complex situation
- Evaluate the conclusions of logical analysis
- Spot solutions that are not obvious
- Forecast and estimate accurately

How Intuition Works
Figure 6 illustrates how intuition works. Your brain subconsciously selects a few vital elements from the situation and from these it forms a pattern which it either recognises from your experience ("aha – that's familiar") or not ("oho – something's wrong"). This is *"perception"*.

You then slot that pattern into existing mental models that you have built up through learning and experience, to form an interpretation of what you have perceived. This is *"understanding"*.

From your understanding, you make a forecast of what will happen next, and use that prediction as the basis for an action plan. This is *"judgement"*. When you commit to that action plan, you have made your decision.

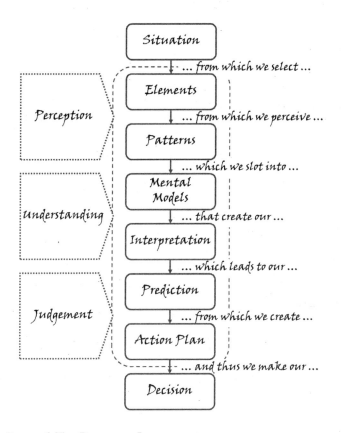

FIGURE 6: THE PROCESS OF INTUITION

Left Brain: Right Brain

There is a lot of nonsense written in popular psychology books about "left brain thinkers" who are logical and analytical, and "right brain thinkers" who are creative and intuitive. This is a shame because there is a sound scientific basis for the location of specific cognitive functions. The issue is that the lateralisation effects are far more complex than it seemed back in 1981 when neuropsychologist Roger Sperry won his Nobel Prize, and scientists are still far from unravelling all of the complexities.

Experiments have shown, however, that the process of describing a situation in words, using primarily the linguistic centres of the left side of your brain, does frustrate your ability to jump to an insightful response based on intuition. Wise problem-solvers and decision-makers must therefore be able to assess which style of thinking will best serve the task at hand.

Intuitive thinking is best for:
- Rapid insight
- Complex and subtle situations
- Poorly-defined and ambiguous problems
- Domains in which you have real depth of experience

Logical thinking is best for:
- Measured analysis to provide a describable justification
- Review and comparison of multiple options
- Computing results using formulae or algorithms
- Domains where you have less experience

When Intuition Fails

Figure 6 details the process of intuitive thinking. From this we can see that if any of the links were to fail, your intuition would let you down. This is illustrated in Figure 7.

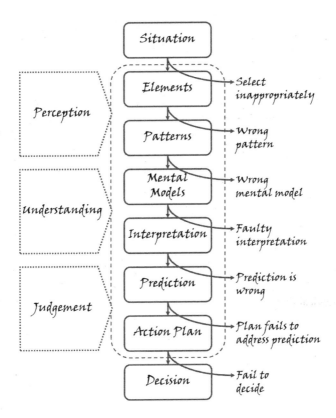

Figure 7: Six Ways Intuition Can Fail You

How to Develop your Intuition

One of the important factors when applying intuitive or logical thinking is your level of experience. This is therefore the key to developing your intuition: acquire real depth of experience. This allows you to select the right cues from what is happening, recognise patterns and build the mental models that will allow you to interpret events.

Develop your Intuition

To achieve wisdom, you need to know your own domain of knowledge intimately and seek out relevant experiences. As your intuition develops, look for opportunities to broaden your domain. Interest yourself in other areas of experience and knowledge too, so that your intuition can harness connections, similarities and analogies.

Seek out chances to make decisions, participate in decision-making or even shadow a decision process – identifying what you *would decide*, were you in the decision-making role.

Before deciding, analyse the nature of the decision:
- What makes it hard or easy?
- What are the potential pitfalls?
- What experience is relevant?

After deciding, review your experience:
- What made it hard or easy?
- What was the sequence of events and considerations you made?
- What cues did you use and how did you interpret them?

Summarise your learning by noting what you would do next time.

DISCRIMINATE PRECISELY

The ultimate goal of honing your perception is to become sensitive to the smallest details that will allow you discriminate precisely between two different things that look, to the unskilled, the same. This will allow you to discern the true meaning of the cues you receive, and to separate the relevant from the background information.

Whether your goal is to find a powerful strategy, to manage people effectively or to monitor and control a situation, there will always be a vital few critical factors that make the difference between ease and difficulty – maybe even between success and failure. If you don't spot these, you will dissipate effort on the wrong things. Using one or two indicators to control a whole system is called *"situational leverage"*.

Interpreting for Others

Wise people often speak in simple terms. They have a talent for articulating complex and subtle concepts with clarity and simplicity. They understand the interconnectedness of things but, with their deep understanding, can discern which features are most essential. They can then use these to build simple models that allow the rest of us to gain a glimpse into reality and feel we have seen clearly and understood.

Pervasiveness and Personalisation

When we discussed Inner Strength in Chapter One, we encountered the two styles of thought: Pervasiveness and Personalisation. Seeing events for what they are will allow you to discriminate which are pervasive and which are transitory; which events cleave to you and your characteristics, and which would happen anyway.

Pervasiveness

Pervasiveness is the belief that things happen to you because that is how the world always is. Humans are highly prone to making patterns of events, so we readily infer pervasiveness from a few unrelated circumstances. We do not notice the background of events that contradict our faulty interpretation. This is sometimes called the *"confirming evidence bias"* – preferentially observing events that confirm our prejudice and not seeing those that would disprove it.

Personalisation

Another form of this trap is the *"ad hominem fallacy"*. When we believe that *"these things always happen to me"* we attribute this, falsely, to *"who I am"*. Again, we need to notice the background of events to create a more accurate understanding.

These examples are reminiscent of the figure-to-ground illusions that give different images depending on whether we focus on the foreground, or the background space.

FIGURE 8: FIGURE TO GROUND ILLUSION

The Smart to Wise Journey

Dr Benjamin Bloom defined three broad domains of learning:

- Cognitive (knowledge)
- Affective (attitudes)
- Psychomotor (physical skills)

He also started work on defining levels of mastery and his model for increasing mastery in the cognitive domain echoes our journey from smart to wise.

Bloom divided it into six levels of increasing mastery. He proposed that the lowest level was simple knowledge and the ability to remember. As we learn further, we rise through successive levels of comprehension (understanding what we know), application (being able to act on our knowledge) and analysis (understanding). His two highest levels of mastery, which we can identify with the emergence of wisdom, are synthesis (creating new knowledge and merging different ideas) and evaluation (a critical assessment of our knowledge).

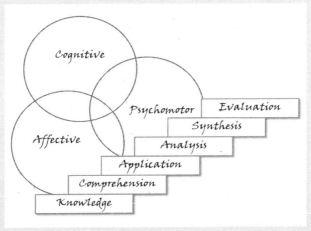

FIGURE 9: BLOOM'S TAXONOMY

Third Pillar:
EVOLUTION

WISDOM AS EXPERIENCE

To what extent is wisdom *merely* a function of age? Some might say that acquiring wisdom is simply a matter of waiting and that it cannot be rushed.

Narrow Wisdom

We could define *"Narrow Wisdom"* as deep expertise in a very narrow domain, such as exceptional skill in playing a musical instrument, tremendous facility with mathematics or the prowess of a great gymnast. Narrow wisdom is often acquired at a young age as a result of extensive, dedicated practice.

The *"narrow is deep"* paradox means that we often carry across our perception of a person's wisdom from the narrow domain into other, wider contexts. This is usually an application of the *"ad hominem fallacy"* in reverse. We apply our knowledge of a person in one context to pre-suppose their abilities in another. While some people are wise in multiple domains, it is risky to simply assume wisdom outside of the domain in which you have observed wisdom.

Wisdom as Maturity

Can we put our finger on an aspect of wisdom that comes with age? Carl Jung certainly did. His concept of *"individuation"* argued that, as we age, we start to integrate the different elements of our personality to achieve a balance. This leaves us more comfortable than the young with uncertainty, and less extreme in our views. We become more focused on understanding events and their significance and less eager for rapid action.

The dividing line, by convention, is a "mid-life crisis" during which we make our last attempts to keep up with the young. This precipitates a move into the second part of our life, in which we focus on finding meaning. Arguably, when we stop trying to be like the young, we start being perceived as "mature".

Experience at the Heart of Wisdom

Striving for meaning in the second part of our lives increases our focus on understanding and learning from experience. In the language of *Smart to Wise,* these two drives are perception (understanding) and evolution (learning). Evolution will require many practical skills.

The Skills of Evolution
1.   Contemplation
2.   Questioning and curiosity
3.   Reflection
4.   Receiving feedback
5.   Connecting with people and discussion
6.   Research
7.   Making connections between ideas and knowledge
8.   Learning and unlearning
9.   Creative problem solving
10. Accepting ambiguity and uncertainty

Fundamentally, evolution is about being open to changing your mind, your attitudes, your behaviours and your thought patterns.

OPEN MIND

An open mind is not an empty mind, any more than an open house is an empty house. The difference is a "welcoming" attitude. It is about being curious to learn new ideas, and also being humble enough to accept that your current knowledge plus your new knowledge does not yet represent full knowledge. In practical terms, you must become comfortable with the answer "I don't know" and be prepared to research, listen and reason, to find more knowledge. You must be prepared to place yourself in the seemingly weak position of asking for advice.

As your knowledge progresses, you must also be ready to unlearn some of the things that have served you well, but that are mere approximations to the truth. This will feel like going backwards. The world is sometimes more subtle and complex than you imagined when you had a lower level of knowledge.

Sometimes wisdom is not in trying to be an expert when you lack expertise, but rather, in interpreting the experts by understanding their knowledge and making it accessible to others.

Beginner's Mind

A key aspect of Buddhism involves having an attitude that is wholly open to new experience, new ideas, new thinking. It is a willingness to set aside prior knowledge and learning and can be illustrated by the following story.

A university professor went to visit a Zen master to learn about Zen. The master first made tea. He poured it into his visitor's cup. And he kept pouring. The professor said, *"Stop! It is full. It can hold no more tea."*

"Indeed," said the master, *"and like this cup, you are full of your own knowledge and opinions. Before you can learn about Zen, you must first empty your cup."*

Twelve Ways to Cultivate an Open Mind

1. Keep a notebook or journal to record new ideas and experiences
2. Read across all areas of knowledge and many genres of fiction
3. Select and read a variety of magazines each month
4. Set aside time to read and time to think

5. Look for connections between the things you learn and the ideas you encounter
6. Take an interest in all areas of culture and news
7. Pay attention to and notice things in your environment
8. Research the things you hear or read about, but do not understand
9. Take things you know and ask yourself "why?" about them
10. Talk to people about their subjects of interest and listen for new ideas
11. Analyse events and commentaries on them for as many different and conflicting explanations as you can find – look for the truth in each
12. Once a month, attend or visit a different cultural event or venue: museums, galleries, concerts, theatre, seminars, lectures, TV or radio recordings, debates…

CURIOSITY

"The more that you read, the more things you will know. The more things that you learn, the more places you'll go."

Dr Seuss: *I Can Read With My Eyes Shut*

Confucius records that, after a day without food and a night without sleep, during which he took time to think, there was no gain. *"Thinking is not as good as studying."* It is during study that you can form new ideas – often in the background, at an unconscious level. Contemplation alone rarely creates new ideas;

it just gives your brain the freedom to become aware of the results of assimilating and synthesising the new ideas that you have absorbed.

Every scrap of knowledge has value, so take every experience as part of your learning and be curious about your surroundings, the people you meet and the events that transpire.

> *"Whatever is interesting we are interested in. Whatever is not interesting, we are even more interested in. Everything is interesting if looked at in the right way."*
> **The QI Philosophy – QI Ltd**

Insatiable curiosity means asking yourself questions all of the time, and sharing them with the people around you to gain the benefits of their insights. Ask: how, where, what, when, who and, above all, why. And to create new ideas, as we'll see soon, ask "what if?".

The Role of Play

Children express their curiosity without reservation. *"Why this, daddy? Why that, mummy?"* are familiar refrains to any parent. As adults, we too easily sublimate our curiosity behind a façade of sophistication. Children satisfy much of their curiosity through play. A step on the route to wisdom is to regain your playfulness and curious child mind. Playing with words, ideas and things is one of the most powerful ways to learn and to acquire the deepest levels of insight.

Networking Tip

As you extend your network of contacts, you expand the breadth of your experiences and the experiences of others that you can tap into. Are you one of the many people who feel uncomfortable at networking events and when you meet new people? Here is the secret to making it fun and also to getting people to like you.

When you go into an environment where you will meet new people, become curious. Make it your mission to learn something new and interesting from everyone you meet. This will have three effects:

1. It will remove the anxiety from having to make small talk.
2. It will allow you to ask questions of other people and encourage them to talk about themselves – to them, the most interesting topic in the world.
3. It will encourage you to listen, making you attractive to others.

Embracing Subtlety

Sometimes the best explanation for something is simple and direct. Most of the time, however, this is not the case. Moving from smart to wise means embracing the complexity and ambiguity of the real world, and learning to accept when a simple answer is insufficient.

Complexity

Our world and the systems that make it up are becoming more complex and more dynamic. Smart minds will look for simple models to help them navigate these complexities, while the weak-minded will put complex systems into a category of "unknowable" and refuse to fully engage with them.

This refusal to engage leads to faith-based positions and the constant occurrence of surprising out-of-the-blue events that we fail to foresee. The wise engage, seek to understand and are able to detect trends. They can still miss salient evidence or misinterpret, but they will more often be prepared. Engage with the new, the complex and the hard-to-understand: do not treat them as objects of fear or faith. These are where the riches lie for the wise.

Ambiguity

> *"**Ambiguity** (n): bearing two or more possible interpretations"*

Ambiguity and doubt are two sides of the same coin; ambiguity demands your humility, but it is also the progenitor of new knowledge and understanding. Hegel's process of dialectic reasoning sees collisions of ideas as fruitful. The resolution of the contradiction between an idea – *"thesis"* – and its opposite – *"antithesis"* – is a new concept, the *"synthesis"*, which opens us up to new insights.

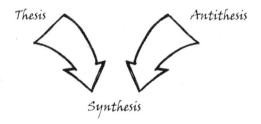

FIGURE 10: HEGELIAN DIALECTIC

In passing, it is worth noting that prominent among the many theories of how humour works is the idea that ambiguity is the necessary precursor. It makes possible the unexpected, the misinterpretation and the misdirection upon which much humour depends.

In other contexts, ambiguity can trigger anxiety. This can be a powerful ally: if you are alert to the signs of your own anxiety, you will pick up the trace of ambiguity before you fall into the trap of simplistic reasoning. Calm yourself using the SCOPE process and then apply your intuition to cut through the complexity to a deeper understanding.

The SCOPE Process

Stop	Pause, take time to reflect. Control your anxiety and refuse to let the ambiguity overwhelm your critical faculties.
Clarify	Look for additional information, ask questions, design tests or experiments to learn more. This may make things seem more complex and ambiguous, but this is a sign you are approaching reality.
Options	What are the ways you can interpret what you have learned and how you can act in response? Evaluate them against all of the evidence.
Proceed	Once you have a decision, act decisively.
Evaluate	Constantly monitor the situation to assess the clarity of your thinking and the appropriateness of your decision. Reevaluate as new evidence surfaces.

In the previous chapter, we saw how important intuition is in perception. It is also one of the most powerful tools for coping with and seeing through ambiguity. In a process that Malcolm Gladwell describes as *"thin-slicing"*, your brain is able to select the salient evidence and interpret it in isolation from the noise – the mass of other, often conflicting, data that obscures the truth. Thin-slicing, however, only works reliably in contexts where you have deep and relevant experience.

Difference

> *"Who is wise? He that learns from every man; for it is said, from all my teachers I gat understanding."*
> **Attributed to Ben Zoma, in Book 4 of *Pirkei Avot***
> **(Sayings of the Fathers)**

It is easy to like and respect people who agree with you, but the wise thing to do is to engage with the widest possible spread of ideas and opinions and to evaluate each on its merits. Embracing diversity is not just wise, it is efficient. Much research shows that diverse groups of people who respect one another are better at solving problems and make better decisions than groups drawn from a shared background.

Gary Klein's Uncertainty Management Worksheet

Gary Klein is a prominent researcher in the field of intuition. He has created a simple tool to help in managing uncertainty. For each situation or project:

1. Write down the sources of your uncertainty.
2. For each, what is the type of uncertainty: missing information, untrustworthy information, too much information, too difficult to interpret?
3. Look for relevant tactics, such as: delaying, gathering more information, experimenting, simplifying, baby steps, contingency planning, accepting the uncertainty.

Growth

"Either you're growing or you're decaying; there's no middle ground."

Alan Arkin

Growing relies upon your willingness to step out of your comfort zone and into the unknown. Taking risks is a means to grow and learn. This means seeking out new experiences, new ideas and new knowledge. Management researcher Robert Kaiser found that the most successful executives were the ones with the widest breadth of experiences – both with people and environments. This is because we are all immensely changeable: if you continually invest in acquiring new knowledge and skills you will continue to change.

"Never take on a job that you can do."
                                        Dame Elizabeth Filkin

Your Strengths are Your Power

In deciding which direction to channel your growth, you have two diametrically opposite alternatives: you can address your weaknesses or feed your strengths. Of course, in the subtle, complex, real world, there is an infinite variety of options, but let's stick with the simple model for now.

Most learning and development programmes are designed to tackle your weaknesses head-on. This is hard work and much psychological research endorses the view that when we argue for our limitations, we strengthen them. We do have real limitations, and we thrive best we are able to exploit our strengths. When we invest in them, we enhance them.

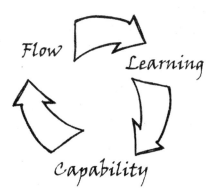

FIGURE 11: BOOTSTRAPPING YOUR STRENGTHS

In Figure 11, you can see the reinforcing feedback loop that you can benefit from when you exercise a strength properly. When you take on challenging work or you practice at your limits in a discipline you enjoy, you enter a *"flow state"* where time passes unnoticed and you feel a deep sense of fulfilment from the task. This creates peak conditions for the learning that will enhance your strength. If you then push yourself a little harder, you will maintain your ability to access a flow state, and thus learn even more, in an effortless way.

Strength-spotting

There are a number of tools to help you identify your strengths, such as the VIA (Values in Action) Signature Strengths survey at http://uat.viacharacter.org or the Gallup Strengths Finder 2.0 in the book of the same name. You could also sit quietly and write down all of the things you have done well – at work, at home and socially. What have people complimented you on? What successes have you had?

Strength-building

Which of these strengths are central to what you do now or what you want to do in the future? Hone your list to around six or seven that you can best invest in to see positive changes. Set yourself challenges that will stretch your current level of capability to higher levels or into a new direction.

Welcoming Failure

> *"To make a mistake and not correct it: this is really what is called a mistake."*
>
> **Confucius, *The Analects***

You learn more from your failures than from your successes, which often pass unexamined. Every mistake can teach you something as long as you welcome failure as a chance to grow. This is not to say, however, that you would be wise in encouraging failure!

Asking Questions

> *"Judge a man by his questions, rather than by his answers."*
>
> **Voltaire**

To evolve as an individual you must become adept at asking questions; of yourself and of others. The measure of quality of a question is what it exposes: knowledge, assumptions, patterns, gaps; even ignorance. Good questions lead to new realisations.

The Questions You Ask

Question everything; be curious about everything. Ask: "*How does this work? Why is this the way it is? How can this change?*" Good questions do not impose assumptions on the world or on the person you ask, but are wide open to gather most information.

We can also use questions to test assumptions and preconceptions. The ancient Greeks had the concept of *"elenchus"*. This was the method Socrates used to examine the beliefs of his pupils, by highlighting contradictions. Use this method on yourself. Ask: "*How do I know this? What is the evidence? What contradicts my understanding or belief?*"

In the dialogues that Plato wrote, Socrates would start with a universal experience such as love or honour and ask what it was. He would then look for counter examples and challenge his pupil with that, to probe more deeply into the meaning and their understanding of the concept. Often, he would demonstrate that what we think we know very well is often not so upon deep examination.

The Connections You Make

Evolution and learning come when we make connections – either between two things we thought were unconnected or between something we knew and something new. The more connections you can make, the more you can perceive the subtlety and complexity of things; and the closer you get to achieving deep understanding.

The Question "Why?"

"Why?" is the most powerful question of all. "Why?" you ask. It puts us into a childlike state of curiosity, and it is never satisfied. It uncovers reasons and is heedless of the consequences. All scientific inquiry is motivated by "why?".

"Why" is also dangerous. When you ask it of somebody, they feel challenged – perhaps even threatened. It probes at their reasons, their values, at what they hold most dear. Ask "why" of the situation, but not of the person.

Finding Root Causes

"Why?" is at the heart of a simple technique to uncover root causes and probe the depths of a situation. The technique is called *"Five Whys"*.

Look at any problem and ask *"Why did this problem happen?"* Often, the answer to the first *"why?"* will prompt another *"why?"* and this answer will prompt another, and so on. Start at the end result and work backward (toward the root cause), continually asking: *"Why?"* Repeat this until the root cause of the problem is apparent.

Why five? Often it is the right number of times to ask *"why?"* – often it is not. Sometimes you will reach the root of the problem with fewer steps; sometimes you need more.

Creativity

Creativity is the source of growth in any culture, as well as the driver for revolutionary change. Your ability to find creative solutions to problems and to innovate will indicate continued flexibility in your thinking that is a necessary component of wisdom.

Do you have Space to Think?

Creativity requires not only that your brain can process new connections, which it can happily do in background, at an unconscious level. It also requires quiet thinking time to allow your new insights and creative ideas to emerge into your conscious mind. Make time in your week for thinking time, when you have no distractions, just time to think about the issue of the moment, or to ponder what is around the next bend.

Solving Problems

> *"The significant problems we have cannot be solved at
> the same level of thinking with which we created them."*
> **Albert Einstein**

The transition from smart to wise is marked by a new way of solving problems. A whole wealth of experiences are deployed in creating a web of connections that can understand a problem in a more holistic way, can see it from wholly different perspectives, and can transform it into something new. Many of the techniques of creative thinking are designed to simulate the connections that experience will offer you by providing external stimuli to connect to the problem.

Innovating

Never be seduced into thinking that because something has always been one way; it must always remain that way.

> *"When a distinguished but elderly scientist states that
> something is possible, he is almost certainly right.
> When he states that something is impossible, he is very
> probably wrong."*
> **Arthur C. Clarke, Clarke's First Law,**
> in ***Profiles of the Future***

Innovation, invention and creation mean escaping the constraints of your usual thought processes and overcoming some constraint in your thinking. This is what "thinking out of the box" means. The boundaries are your beliefs, habitual patterns of thinking and the norms you have become used to. New ideas and experiences are what shake these up.

Wisdom and Intelligence

Wisdom and intelligence are clearly different things, but research into intelligence suggests the hint of a meaningful link.

General Intelligence (G)

Researchers divide general intelligence (G) into a vast array of cognitive skills, from verbal to visual, to mathematical, to reasoning, but these skills are fundamentally divided into two clusters: Fluid Intelligence (Gf), which involves reasoning and problem solving, and Crystallised Intelligence (Gc), which is about acquired knowledge and abilities. The patterns of how we develop and maintain these two forms of intelligence are very different and hint at the distinction between smart and wise.

Gf and Gc are not the whole story by far, but they do stand for clusters of characteristics that behave in distinct ways.

Fluid Intelligence (Gf)

Fluid intelligence appears to be largely biologically determined – a function of genetic and environmental factors such as health and injury. It develops rapidly during childhood and adolescence and reaches a peak in the late teens or early twenties. From then on, the decline is steady and significant. Currently, evidence suggests that while physical exercise and healthy behaviours can slow the decline in Gf, "brain training" has little or no effect on the decline. Aging and dementia do, however, appear to be reduced in those who regularly take on complex cognitive tasks, creating a greater "cognitive reserve". This suggests that while out-of-the-box systems may not work, continuing to learn and interact socially across a wide range of intellectual activities can slow the decline of your fluid intelligence.

Crystallised Intelligence (Gc)

Crystallised intelligence also rises during our early years, but it continues to rise. While the increase slows down in our mid years, we appear to be able to cultivate Gc indefinitely, up to the point where physiological factors such as disease or injury physically destroy this ability. It is crystallised intelligence that gives us the breadth of knowledge that we need to discern patterns, make connections and assess complex patterns.

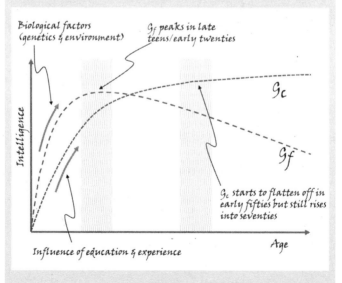

FIGURE 12: HOW GF AND GC VARY WITH AGE

Smart and Wise

My hypothesis is that we are at our smartest near to the peak of fluid intelligence – we are able to reason well and have acquired a good deal of knowledge and experience about the world we live in. As Gf declines, we may become poorer at solving novel problems, but our increasing knowledge and understanding add a new dimension. This access to greater knowledge can compensate and those who cultivate a growth in crystallised intelligence, while managing to retain as much of their flexible Gf capacity as possible, will be the ones who are widely perceived as wise. Modern neuroscience is demonstrating that there is no reason why our brains cannot be as able at 60 as they are at 16. Constant learning, social activities and varied problem solving and reasoning can allow us, like great thinkers of the past, to retain our intellectual powers well into old age.

Fourth Pillar:
CONDUCT

WISDOM AS VIRTUE

What is the relationship between wisdom and virtue?

The two concepts have always been intimately entwined. The ancient Chinese had, as a part of their concept of wisdom, *Te* or "natural virtue". *Te* was not a moral virtue, but an inner feeling of what is the right way to leave nothing undone – following the flow, or the *Tao*. For the wise person, *Te* is their way of doing the right thing because it is right and not because it is virtuous. *Te* lies in deep skills, polished craft and effortless precision.

The collected instructional guidance now known as the Old Testament's Book of Proverbs collates ideas from across the ancient near east, and frequently links the two concepts, as it does at Chapter 8, verse 12: *"I am Wisdom, I bestow shrewdness and show the way to knowledge and prudence."* In the more poetic language of the King James Version, the link is clearer still: *"I wisdom, dwell with prudence."*

Prudence means a cautious, literally "far-sighted", approach to practical affairs.

Finally, near the start of western Philosophy, Aristotle defined – among nine intellectual virtues – *Sophia,* or wisdom. So wisdom is a virtue. It grants you the ability to choose the right thing to do.

The Aristotelian Intellectual Virtues

The five primary intellectual virtues: the virtues of thought

Sophia	Wisdom
Episteme	Empirical and scientific knowledge
Nous	Intellect, reasoning and intuition
Phronesis	Practical wisdom
Techne	Technical wisdom, skill, art and craft

Aristotle also mentions four lesser intellectual virtues

Eubolia	Deliberating well
Sunesis	Understanding and insight
Gnome	Judgement, consideration and persuasion
Deinotes	Cleverness – or maybe "Smartness"

And when you do the wrong thing, Wisdom still gives you the opportunity to do right by acknowledging your error openly and changing direction. As American folk advice would have it, when you are wrong: *" 'fess-up, say sorry, put it right and move on."*

GOOD CONDUCT

Good conduct is about making the right choices about what to do. It is therefore inextricably defined by your ethical and moral compass, and driven by the strength of your determination to follow where it points. Fundamentally, what you do will determine who you are.

Ethics and Morality

It would be unwise to try to list a set of moral or ethical principles that could be universally perceived as wise. Centuries of philosophers have tried. Wisdom is, perhaps, studying these principles and building your own synthesis. A flawed approach would be to accept a moral or ethical code that was simply given to you or, worse, imposed on you by some element of your society or upbringing. We must each challenge received ideas and find our own way; an authentic morality and ethical code.

Immanuel Kant had a go at creating a universal rule of morality; his *categorical imperative*. This states that you should:

> *"Act only according to such principles that you would wish to be universal laws."*

Kant believed that if any moral choice were to be valid, we must have a genuine choice: true compulsion leads to neither moral nor immoral acts. Later philosophers have built on this, codifying one form of ethical behaviour that is universally respected across all human cultures: that of personal responsibility.

It may sometimes be smart to try and wriggle out of responsibility for an action, but it is only when you take responsibility that you regain control.

Blame

Events and the actions of others can sometimes restrict your choices in life, leaving you feeling that you are not in control. The usual response in these circumstances is to blame your predicament on someone or something else. Blame leaves you feeling absolved of the responsibility. But this is neither smart nor wise. Focus instead on your choices and the control that you can assert. *"Blame,"* says the character Louis Dega, in *Papillon* by Henri Charriere, *"is for god and small children."*

Mental Discipline

> *"The truth of the matter is that you always know the right thing to do. The hard part is doing it."*
>
> **General H. Norman Scharzkopf**

Good conduct is as much about mental discipline as it is about the physical courage to do what is right in the face of danger. When something is difficult, unpleasant or just dull, it takes will to motivate yourself to do it. Yet this is an investment in the future.

Psychologist Philip Zimbardo has recently studied how people mentally orient themselves to the past, the present and the future. He discovered that future-oriented people, who are best able to prioritise tasks that will only bear fruit in the future, are more successful and healthier than others who mentally dwell in the present moment or in the past. What they must avoid is the temptation to sacrifice all pleasure and present fulfilment, for a future that therefore never arrives. He also found that those with a positive attitude to their past – valuing its pleasures and learning from its troubles – are the most happy and contented. Zimbardo's research shows us that, once again, wisdom can be found through balance.

The Noble Eight-fold Path

One of the core philosophies in Buddhism is that of *"The Noble Eight-fold Path"*; the route to liberation from suffering and to awakening.

The eight-fold path is organised into three Divisions, which adherents work upon simultaneously. These are: Wisdom (Prajna), Morality (Sila), and Concentration – or meditation (Samadhi). In Buddhism, wisdom and conduct are deeply connected, forming a cycle that leads its adherents to greater enlightenment.

Wisdom

- Right understanding
- Right intentions

Wisdom motivates us to morality

Morality

- Right speech
- Right action
- Right livelihood

Greater morality improves concentration

Concentration

- Right effort
- Right mindfulness
- Right meditation

Concentration deepens wisdom

SELF-CONTROL

If wisdom is a virtue, can we also look at other virtues to discern the components of wisdom? Many cultures have an explicit list of virtues, such as the familiar western concept of the four cardinal virtues of temperance, prudence, courage and justice.

Self-control features prominently in many lists, with virtues like temperance, patience, integrity, perseverance, endurance, discipline, tenacity and restraint. You will find these in modern and ancient lists from India, China, Japan, the Middle and Near East, and Europe.

Discretion

Discretion is about making choices that avoid future problems or embarrassment and the word stems from the same root as discreet (discernment) rather than discrete (separate).

For example, wisdom lies in deciding when to speak and when to stay silent. The politician, scientist, author, diplomat and polymath, Benjamin Franklin, tried to live by 13 virtues of moral perfection that he listed in his notebook. Number two was *"Silence"*:

> *"Speak not but what may benefit others or yourself; avoid trifling conversation."*

Ludwig Wittgenstein returned to the same sentiment, but focused on not exceeding the limits of our knowledge: *"Whereof one cannot speak, thereof one must remain silent."*

When you want to contribute to a discussion, a debate or a decision process, use discretion and adapt the method taught by the US Marine Corps for marksmanship to ensure that your contribution is right on target.

BRASS
As taught in Marksmanship training by the
US Marine Corps

Breathe	This involves taking the time to assess the situation and refresh your mind.
Relax	Calm your mind so that over-eagerness does not diminish the power of your contribution.
Aim	Determine what you will say or do.
Slack	Taking up the slack so that you are ready – weighing your arguments before making them out loud, considering which will have the greatest impact, and how to sequence and present them.
Squeeze	Making your contribution calmly and confidently, without rushing.

Getting the Balance Right

Discretion is also about getting the balance right in your life: in your work, your social life and relationships, and in the way you look after yourself. This is illustrated in Figure 13 on the following page.

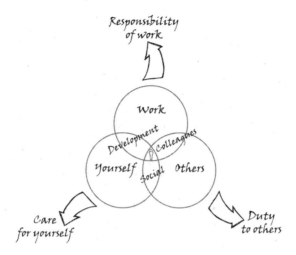

FIGURE 13: BALANCING PRIORITIES

Aggression

Competition can be a valuable route for developing wisdom, yet it can get out of hand and lead to aggressive behaviour that is neither smart nor wise. You must know when to compete, when not to compete and, crucially, when to stop competing. This is the hardest, because the momentum of competition can cloud your judgement, yet it is precisely when your judgement is obscured that it is vital to stop.

Anger

Never let your emotions run so far out of control that you become angry. Genuine anger serves no purpose; its emotion impedes discretion and fairness.

> *"How much more grievous are the consequences of anger than the causes of it."*
>
> **Marcus Aurelius**

In the chapter on Evolution, we discussed the role of maturity in gaining wisdom. One factor is the change in the way your brain responds to perceived threats. In those over 60 years of age, the amygdala (responsible for processing emotional responses) interacts more with the dorsolateral prefrontal cortex (responsible for social and intellectual judgement). This suggests that experience and age lead us to better control of our emotional responses.

The SCOPE Process

You can use the SCOPE process to intervene in an emotional response and drive your reaction towards the reasoning part of your brain.

The SCOPE Process

Stop	Force yourself to pause when confronted with an emotional challenge. Focus on your breathing for a few slow breaths, making each one a little slower more calm.
Clarify	Take time to clarify what you really know. This analysis will distract your emotional response and give you a sounder basis from which to proceed. Also clarify the outcome you want to achieve.
Options	Determine what alternatives are available to you and decide which offers the greatest chance of achieving the outcome you want.
Proceed	Calmly proceed with the strategy you have determined.
Evaluate	Continuously monitor the situation and be prepared to Stop, Clarify and reassess your Options if you are not succeeding in your aim.

Stress

Sustained anger can lead to stress – adverse psychological or physical reactions to sustained pressure. You need to keep your stress levels low in order to exercise wisdom because its effects will compromise your judgement. And because the long term physical effects of stress can be very damaging indeed, it is wise to actively manage your day-to-day stress levels.

Mostly, stress responses are triggered by a feeling that one or more parts of your life are outside of your control. Therefore, the secret to stress management is to take control in all aspects of your life.

How to Take Control

1. Take control of your physical wellbeing with good food, exercise, and relaxation.

2. Take control of your physical environment by managing the space around you and the way your senses are stimulated.

3. Take control of your social life by choosing whom you associate with and relating to them on your own terms.

4. Take control of your attitudes by objectively evaluating the values you live by and the beliefs that limit your choices.

5. Control the way you use your time by prioritising wisely, planning your days and reviewing your priorities frequently.

6. Control your mental response to stressful situations by valuing the resources you have, and focusing on how best to deploy them.

DETERMINATION

We can see determination as a branch of self-control. Of the virtues we listed at the start of that section, those that were particularly valued in Roman society were *disciplina* (discipline), *constantia* (perseverance) and *firmitas* (tenacity).

It would not, however, be wise to pursue these virtues for their own sake. Disciplined conformity to bad rules may be smart, but it is not wise. Perseverance with a lost cause may be noble, but it is not smart. And holding tenaciously to a flawed idea is not noble: it is foolish.

There is therefore an intimate relationship between determination and judgement: you must know when to stop and you must constantly review a situation with total objectivity.

Persistence

Persistence, in the face of opposition and challenge when you know what is right, is a virtue. It is also wise when you foresee a substantial outcome resulting from your determination to succeed. While the virtue of fortitude is often interpreted as "physical courage", it is also the mental and emotional courage to keep going when others would stop, often in the face of criticism, rejection and ridicule.

> *"I am more resolute because all have denied me, than I could ever have been had all accepted me."*
>
> **Walt Whitman**

Perseverance is the outward manifestation of inner resilience – the strength of will that allows you to accept setbacks without losing the confidence that you can continue, or the determination to do so. Will you stand by a friend in need, wrestle with a problem until it is solved, or refuse to accept failure?

Do Things Right

It is easy to draw the distinction that wisdom lies in doing the
right things, while smart is merely doing things right. However,
this is not just trite: it is wrong. As you progress from smart to
wise, you will not only be more adept at choosing the right things
to do, you will also become more astute in assessing how to do
them well. The Taoist concept of *Te* is exemplified by effortless
precision in craft.

To do things right means rejecting established processes and
structures in favour of solving each problem afresh – seeing what
distinguishes it from other situations. It also means discerning the
similarities that you can learn from and the connections you can
make. This requires perception. Create the right process, and then,
when you follow it diligently, it will lead you to the right result.

How to Do Things Right
A Ten-Step Process

1. Determine what success looks like.
2. Identify threats and problems.
3. Inventory your resources – people, knowledge, assets, materials.
4. Create a plan – include activities, sequence, timing, resources, contingencies.
5. Create checklists and cross-checks to help monitor and evaluate progress.
6. Communicate your plan to anyone who needs to participate.
7. Monitor and control your progress, using your checks to assure quality.

8. If something goes wrong, acknowledge it openly, re-evaluate and re-plan. Be prepared to abort.
9. Maintain frequent and effective communication.
10. Evaluate outcomes, recognise contribution, celebrate success and analyse lessons learnt.

GENEROSITY

It is perhaps unsurprising that the religious codes of ethics from around the world emphasise the virtues of generosity: *dana* (generosity) in Buddhism, altruism in Hinduism and charity in the Abrahamic religions (Judaism, Christianity and Islam). Generosity is a virtue for its own sake. It is also wise, for three reasons.

1. The pragmatic reason is the power of our instinct to reciprocate. When we receive a gift, a favour or a concession, we feel an obligation which leads to an "economy" based on the reciprocation of these exchanges. It seems likely that the universal nature of trading in human societies is based in this compulsion. Generosity allows you to create a bank of favours owed.
2. However, it is more than just truism to note that generosity repays the giver more directly. When we give something to another person, we learn from the experience and value the way we feel. Generosity will reduce your stress levels and make you feel good by giving you a sense of control.
3. Finally, generosity builds your reputation. When you choose what and how to give wisely, your generosity becomes a tool to communicate your wisdom.

Material Generosity

Generosity with your resources; be they assets or materials, your knowledge and experience, or simply your time, can all be grouped together as material generosity – the giving of something that has tangible value. Rarely does this have to be gifts of wealth, as in the days of feudal monarchs demonstrating power through the splendour of their generosity.

Personal Generosity

One of the ways we adjudge people as wise is through the others whom they support and develop. A special form of material generosity is the giving of that which is most valuable – your time. Wise people create networks of friendships to whom they give their time without reservation. They provide first class opportunities for smart colleagues and friends to observe them, participate in their affairs and learn from them.

Spiritual Generosity

The other form of generosity reflects virtues that we have not yet examined: tolerance, forgiveness and mercy. Many spiritual traditions see this as a primary route to renouncing the physical constraints of life and achieving spiritual enlightenment through a chain of:

Tolerance – Compassion – Mercy – Forgiveness – Selflessness

In a more secular sense, selflessness is an admirable goal in your transformation from smart to wise. It is always smart to look after yourself. But this leads to a bias towards subjectivity that must, necessarily, block access to true perception and good judgement, and therefore to wisdom. When you put yourself and your personal needs and desires to one side, you regain your objectivity.

Practical Wisdom

Practical wisdom is the application of sound judgement to practical matters. It allows you to conceive of what a good life, a sound strategy or an effective process is, and it provides the practical skills to deliver them. The ancient Greeks distinguished between Phronesis – practical wisdom – and Sophia – wisdom in abstract philosophical matters. Aristotle believed phronesis to be necessary for one to be considered virtuous.

While being smart requires you to understand how the world works; being wise demands experience to understand beyond the ideal, theoretical world, to accurately interpret the context. Practical wisdom is concerned with these particulars, so that you can discern both what is right and how to act correctly. Samuel Taylor Coleridge described practical wisdom perfectly:

"Common sense in an uncommon degree is what the world calls wisdom."

Fifth Pillar:
JUDGEMENT

JUDGEMENT AS THE PRODUCT OF CHARACTER

Judgement is widely associated with wisdom, particularly in the context of the law. It is also associated with the virtue of prudence, the ability to exercise good judgement, reasoning and appropriate caution.

Judgement starts to form the second tier of our pillars of wisdom, because it – along with fairness and authority – rests on the first four. Prudent judgement rests upon:

1. Your moral and ethical code, your value system, your ability to detach yourself from subjective considerations and your authenticity: Self-mastery

2. Your ability to understand the situation, discerning the true nature of things and their meaning in the context: Perception
3. Tacit knowledge gathered from experience and an ability to question what is before you with an open mind: Evolution
4. Self-control, discretion and mental discipline, coupled with a compassionate generosity of spirit: Conduct

One could argue that, together, these four pillars form the basis for *character,* the combination of qualities and traits that define you.

FIGURE 14: SEVEN PILLARS

The Greek philosopher, Heraclitus, who took a particular interest in how things change, notably said: *"Character is destiny."*

By this he may have meant that everything you have learnt and all of the choices you have made along the way will inform the choices you make further along your path; and these will determine where that path leads.

Ability to Reason

Reasoning is arguably the key edge that humanity achieved over competing species. Using this ability well is a mark of wisdom and it requires you to develop three values:

1. Scepticism

Scepticism links closely to perception. When you acquire this value, you will prize truth highly enough to question everything with an open mind, taking great care to collect evidence from all sources and evaluate it objectively.

2. Rigour

The rigour of your analysis will determine the ultimate value of your reasoning. You must be prepared to incorporate all evidence and eschew shortcuts that leap over relevant knowledge. This takes patience and care.

3. Courage

Sometimes the conclusions you draw will not be comfortable for you or for others. You must be prepared to defend your conclusions in the face of criticism (yet with and open mind) and act on them with determination.

Rationality

Rationalism is a philosophical approach that seeks out knowledge from pure reasoning: in contrast to *empiricism,* which seeks it in experience. Both reject unquestioning appeals to authority. *Rationality* combines the two, looking for knowledge based in experience and extending it by reasoning.

Philosophers have sought logical modes of reasoning that allow us to determine whether a statement is true or false, based on some premise. In the twentieth century, Kurt Gödel showed that, within a formal system such as mathematics or logic, there will always be some statements of which the truth cannot be decided, such as: *"This statement is false."*

For most of us living and working outside of academic logic and mathematics, however, what matters is that we are able to question evidence, and to reason reliably from it.

Deduction

Deduction is the process of starting with a known truth and demonstrating that it necessarily implies that something else is true. Arthur Conan Doyle's famous fictional detective, Sherlock Holmes, used deductive reasoning to solve crimes. An example might be:

1. "The tyre marks only match the P32X tyre."
2. "The only car that has wheels which the P32X fits is a Model 88."
3. "Therefore the car that made the tracks was a Model 88."

There are two measures of the quality of a deduction: its validity and its soundness. Pure rationalists would assert a statement to be true (valid) if the reasoning is logically correct and statement 3 must necessarily follow from statements 1 and 2. However, it is only sound if it is both valid and based on true assumptions – in our example, if statements 1 and 2 are both necessarily true.

Sadly, however, too many people mistake deduction for its less rigorous cousin, *induction.*

Induction

Induction is the process by which we infer a fact from something we know to be true, because all of the evidence currently available supports it. It remains possible though, that the supposed fact can be falsified by further evidence. In our example, if there is only one set of tyre tracks, we may infer that the criminal drove a Model 88.

As in true scientific reasoning, we must treat the induction as a hypothesis, and seek to verify or falsify it. If, for example, we later discover a footprint in the drive, this opens up a new possibility – that the criminal arrived on foot.

The Confirming Evidence Trap

A common bias in our thinking is to look for evidence to confirm our hypothesis. Indeed, we are psychologically pre-disposed to notice this evidence and not so easily spot evidence that contradicts our beliefs. The nature of induction, however, means that the most valuable evidence is that which can challenge your inference, especially when no amount of confirming evidence can logically generate a deductive proof.

Weight of evidence is often a test we apply, but it can never constitute a formal proof. All of our bias and prejudice flows from not noticing small – and sometimes large – counter-examples.

> *"All swans are white."* Noticing more white swans does not make this statement any truer. Neither does failing to notice any black swans. Seeing one black swan would prove it false. Think about some your beliefs and prejudices. Are they of this nature? What disconfirming evidence are you failing to notice or take heed of?

Abduction

Abduction is an even less robust means of drawing a conclusion. It seeks a cause that explains the evidence, such as *"All criminals drive a Model 88"*. This too is merely a hypothesis, and the only test of an abductive reason is that it is merely plausible. The philosopher Charles Pierce, who introduced the term, described it as *"guessing"*.

Beware how easy it is to become seduced by an argument because it is plausible: it conforms to your existing knowledge – or belief – about how the world works and therefore appears to explain something. Psychologists describe this effect as the *"representativeness bias"*. We interpret events in terms of "typical patterns" – most commonly discounting factors such as coincidence in favour of causation. An important distinction to make is this: *"Correlation does not imply causation."*

We cannot assume that simply because two things occur together, one has caused the other. This is beautifully illustrated by one of fiction's finest deductive minds: John Le Carré's George Smiley.

"It had long been one of Smiley's cardinal principles… not to proceed beyond the evidence. A fact, once logically arrived at, should not be extended beyond its natural significance."

Faith

The poorest form of thinking is neither rational nor empirical: it is faith. Accepting a statement based solely on the authority of the teller – be they an expert or an ancient text – is neither smart nor wise. Such *"magical thinking"* is most common in people who trust in luck. Never let luck be your friend – it is fickle and unreliable, and really just a euphemism for blind chance. The wise course is to commit to reason, exploration, preparation, organisation and hard work. Without these "hope" is just a form of faith and poor judgement.

Faith and Hope are not the same as True Optimism

Some will say that there will be circumstances that you cannot influence, and that in these cases, hope is better than fear or despair. Indeed it is. But where you have evaluated the situation and are certain that no form of action remains open to you then, for the wise, hope becomes *"optimism"*. Not a glass-half-full type of faith-based optimism, but an optimism that remains open to opportunities that the changing situation will present, so that you are ready to once again seize some control. Tune your perception and maintain your flexibility.

Challenging Abductive, Inductive and Faith-Based Reasoning

Two questions will help you expose these kinds of faulty reasoning.

1. You can test causal reasoning by asking a question like: *"By what mechanism does A cause the observed outcome B?"*

2.   You can test an inferred meaning to events by asking a
     question such as: *"What is the demonstrable connection between
     circumstance A and your interpretation, B?"*

Creating a Logical Argument

The Sophists of ancient Greece, and particularly Gorgias, were
derided by Socrates for their willingness to build a compelling
argument around any proposition, true or false. Socrates, however,
did not deride the rhetorical skills that they used to build and
present their arguments.

In wisdom, it is not enough to know the truth: you must
be able to persuade others. Think of the mythical Cassandra,
whose prophecies were always right, but she was fated never to
be believed. It is therefore hugely valuable to learn the skills of
critical reasoning and building arguments. Here are six of them.

1.   Establish a clear link between your premise (something
     your audience will readily accept as true because you have
     established it as fact, or because it is common knowledge)
     and your conclusion (something that flows logically from
     your premise).
2.   Put your ideas into a sequence that makes it easy for your
     audience to follow. Build your argument one step at a time.
3.   Limit the reasons in support of your conclusions to one, two
     or three at most. Paradoxically, the more reasons you give the
     weaker your argument appears to be. However, when citing
     examples in support of an argument, ensure you have several
     and that they are robust.
4.   Ensure that your examples and analogies are relevant and
     representative of the context you are considering.
5.   Use informed and impartial sources, and be sure to check
     them with care.

6. Consider the objections yourself. If you can reject them rigorously, you will rob them of their power to sway your audience.

The Stoic Tradition

An important stage in Western Philosophy was the emergence of the Stoics in the early third century BCE. Their core philosophical starting point was that there is no authority higher than reason. The Stoics were heavily influenced by Heraclitus, whom we met at the start of this chapter. He argued that while nature is supreme, it is governed by principles that we can understand through rational thought. The Stoics saw all emotions as leading to subjective judgements that may be true or false, and thus sought to subject emotion, in turn, to reason so that our judgements will be true.

In this they were anticipating many centuries of intellectual struggle to understand why people's choices are not always rational. In recent years, with financial and trading markets failing, this has come into sharp focus. Traditional economic thinking in the nineteenth and early twentieth centuries had seen markets as the product of many rational choices. We now know that this is not just an over-simplification: it is wrong.

So wisdom requires us to not just reject subjective, faulty and irrational thinking in ourselves, but also to anticipate and understand it in the people around us.

ABILITY TO WEIGH

Your ability to weigh alternatives against one another is the essence of judgement. The now traditional personification of justice is a blindfolded woman with the sword of truth in one hand and the scales of justice in the other.

The blindfold suggests that judgement is blind to all but the facts and, as we will see at the end of the chapter, her sword represents not her power, but her ability to make a judgement. Her scales weigh the reasons.

Can your judgements ever be purely objective? As you move from smart to wise, the questions you are asked to resolve will become increasingly complex and rooted in the human world. Wholly fact-driven judgements can be made relatively easily.

To resolve rational yet value-laden questions requires the wisdom to weigh subjective social considerations against one another, alongside objective facts. This gives rise to what social scientist Bent Flyvbjerg refers to as *"phronetic judgements"*. To make these judgements, he advocates asking four questions:

- Where are we going?
- Who gains and who loses, by which mechanisms of power?
- Is this development desirable?
- What should we do about it?

Critical Thinking

> *"Take nothing on its looks: take everything on the evidence. There is no better rule."*
>
> **The Lawyer, Jaggers, in Charles Dickens'**
> ***Great Expectations***

Critical thinking is the skill that allows us to evaluate evidence and reasoning. It has two principle components, credibility and analysis.

1. Credibility

As Jaggers implies, judgement must start with the facts and your ability to critically distinguish them from appearances of fact. What is the credibility of the information you are working from, and of its source? Multiple sources lend credibility to information – but only if they are truly independent of one another. As an example, many sources on the internet copy information from each other, creating multiple instances of the same error or apocryphal story. Yet, in particular, how much can you trust the credibility of one individual?

Ironically, a relevant quotation frequently attributed to US Senator, Daniel Patrick Moynihan, cannot be reliably sourced. It is near identical to sayings attributed to financier Bernard Baruch and to politician James Schlesinger:

> *"Everyone is entitled to their own opinions, but they are not entitled to their own facts."*

2. Analysis

Use analysis to understand how an argument can be developed and recognise the techniques that are used to make it persuasive. This will enable you to both develop your arguments and evaluate the validity of those that you hear. Are analogies sound? Is evidence used fairly? Is the logic consistent? Have statistics been analysed correctly, using appropriate methods? What happens when you remove appeals to authority, tradition, popularity or emotion? Are correlation and causation confused? How valid are generalisations? Are the arguments self-justifying (or "circular")?

Without the ability to think critically, phronetic judgements become impossible: your assessment of the subtle emotional and social contexts will be easily manipulated by misleading evidence or faulty reasoning.

Know when to say "no"

Saying "yes" to everything is far from wise. You must therefore cultivate the ability to say "no"; to assess when a request or an opportunity is either harmful, unimportant or a distraction from something more important.

This assessment is about where to invest your time, effort and energy to achieve the most that you can, yet retain a balance in your life. Success is rarely about what you choose to do, so much as what you allow yourself to let go of. Former US Secretary of State, Henry Kissinger, said:

> *"Don't be too ambitious. Do the most important thing you can think of doing every year and then your career will take care of itself."*

Decisions are often based on short-term judgements. As part of your critical thinking, think about the lifetime cost and value of a potential decision. How would you be able to assess your choice in fifty years' time? This is not to argue that short-term considerations are irrelevant; lifetime cost/value informs an additional, strategic perspective on a decision, negotiation or relationship.

The Human Dimension: Social and Political Considerations

The last of our seven pillars will be authority: your ability to influence and use your wisdom to change other people's thinking. Never let your ego get in the way of your decisions, nor pick a fight for the sake of it: choose the fights that you can win, and choose the fights that you must fight, but walk away from all others. You must always understand and respect the power balance, to make a phronetic judgement.

You must also understand the things that matter most to people. Rudolph Giuliani, Mayor of New York during the 11 September 2001 attacks, recognised this. He articulated a political judgement that guided him: "weddings discretionary: funerals mandatory".

ABILITY TO FORECAST

In his 2005 book *Expert Political Judgement*, Philip Tetlock analysed over 82,000 forecasts by experts against the actual outcomes. They barely out-performed the predictions of informed non-experts, or random chance. J Scott Armstrong, a marketing professor, had earlier proposed his *"seer-sucker theory"* that:

> *"No matter how much evidence exists that seers don't exist, suckers will pay for the existence of seers."*

Tetlock's analysis did find a very valuable result. He divided his experts into "foxes" and "hedgehogs", taking the distinction from a fragment of seventh century BCE poetry from Greek poet Archilochus: *"the fox knows many things, but the hedgehog knows one big thing"*. Tetlock found that foxes usually perform better than hedgehogs at forecasting events. With a single narrow focus, hedgehogs can be blind to the subtle interactions outside their area of specialism, and are also more easily seduced by the depth of their expertise into over-confidence.

Ironically, it is the hedgehogs with their didactic certainty who are most often called upon to comment in the media. Competing hedgehog points of view create the kind of adversarial debate that makes exciting viewing or listening, but rarely exposes the subtle nuances of a situation.

Embrace Complexity

Wisdom requires you to eschew extremities of hedgehog positions and seek out the difficult, challenging complexities of a situation. Simple answers to complex issues are seductive but rarely correct: there are no magic bullets. If you reject binary choices, you must engage in the subtlety and sophistication of the details. There will lie the real insights. The fox, by knowing many things, has access to the wider variety of influences and ideas.

This is one of the reasons why studying and continuing to study the liberal arts – literature, history, science, languages and philosophy – are vital parts of your journey from smart to wise. They will encourage you to see the world in all of its complexity and understand the subtle interplay of many inter-connected factors. It will help you to become a fox.

Planning Fallacy

All plans are wrong. As soon as they are created, the universe will shift the ground and they become out of date. The *"planning fallacy"* is a failure to recognise this essential truth, and instead, to believe your plans. At best, a plan is no more than a good approximation to what will happen if all of your assumptions turn out to be correct. In particular, the term was first coined by psychologists Daniel Kahneman and Amos Tversky to refer to our tendency to underestimate how long something will take, even in the presence of our experience that similar tasks have overrun in the past.

The *"law of unintended consequences"* means that you can never foresee all of the consequences of an action. The law should tell you that your actions may create results that you had not planned for. Your most valuable assets, therefore, are scepticism and flexibility. Doubt your own plans and create options for the future.

The Wisdom of Crowds

Forecasting is often improved by the presence of multiple forecasters. In his book *The Wisdom of Crowds,* James Surowiecki identifies three criteria for a group to outperform individuals:

1. Independence

Each group member must think independently to prevent mistakes from being correlated. Ideally, each new individual brings new information and there is a reduction in the effect of peer pressure to agree with one another on the simple aspects of the problem, and thus avoid its complexities.

2. Diversity

Different perspectives are important; they make it easier for individuals to contribute opinions and to challenge others' thinking. Research shows that adding people who know less, but have different skills, improves a group's performance, and that *"the presence of a minority viewpoint, all by itself, makes a group's decisions more nuanced and its decision making process more rigorous".*

3. De-centralisation

There must be no overall control over data gathering but instead, a means of effectively collating diverse data and making it available for each individual to interpret separately.

Philip Tetlock suggests a way to aggregate the views of experts to understand their forecasts and create a better prediction. Add the forecasts of four foxes, plus two hedgehogs at opposite ends of the spectrum (say, pessimistic and optimistic), to create an average and statistical spread. Add the forecasts and divide by six, for a mean forecast, and subtract the smallest (hedgehog) estimate from the largest and divide by six to get an estimate of the standard deviation. This mirrors the PERT (Program Evaluation and Review Technique) method that project managers sometimes use to estimate the duration of project activities.

ABILITY TO DECIDE

When you review problem solving methodologies and models, you will find a vital step missing from many of them: decision. Deciding what to do is the gateway to action. Our word "decision" comes from the Latin *"de caedere"*, to cut off from. Lady Justice's sword of truth is there to separate the right from the wrong – to choose.

Decision Process

> *"Measure twice – cut once."*
>
> **A proverb learnt from my father**

One of the risks of intuitive thinking, which we discussed under perception, is that it is based on pattern recognition and a mental model. If you sense an irrelevant pattern or apply an inappropriate mental model, then a bad decision will follow. A decision process is therefore a valuable tool to help keep your decisions sound.

Some factors should raise alarms, such as self-interest, emotional attachments or unusual experiences that are likely to be unrepresentative of more common situations. When these factors are present, it is wise to compare your intuitive preferences with the result of a structured decision process. You will get valuable insights when you explore the differences and are able to understand the reasons. When the two match up, you can feel a greater measure of confidence.

A Structured Decision Process

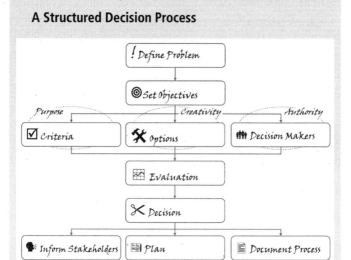

FIGURE 15: STRUCTURED DECISION PROCESS

In Figure 15, six steps precede the decision itself.

1. Define the Problem

What, exactly, is the problem? Have you seen it before? What evidence is available? Collect data from what has happened and devise tests to establish the facts. Gather background information on who the interested parties ("stakeholders") are, and their interests in the problem and its resolution.

2. Set Objectives

Define the objectives for successful resolution. What outcomes do you want?

3. Criteria

Establish the criteria against which you will evaluate any potential solution.

4. Options

Find as many options as you can for a potential resolution. You may then reduce these by applying some "quick criteria" to establish some options that are evidently not sustainable. Do this with care.

5. Authority

Who will make the decision? Do they have the legitimate and intellectual authority to make a sound decision?

6. Evaluation

Apply your criteria rigorously to your options to get a ranking of possible solutions. Your decision must be based on that ranking, but not necessarily determined by it. One of your criteria may have been to accept the ranking as the sole driver of your decision. Equally, you may choose to allow yourself the option to override the ranking by applying intuition at this stage.

Decisions and Action

As we have seen, a good decision requires a sound diagnosis, effective criteria to guide you and a fair evaluation of options against those criteria. It also requires coherent action following a credible plan. To not plan – or worse, to not act – will render any decision ineffective. It can never be falsified nor validated, and so remains just a theoretical exercise. As soon as you know what you need to do, create a plan and get started. You must never shy away from the responsibility that your decisions create for you.

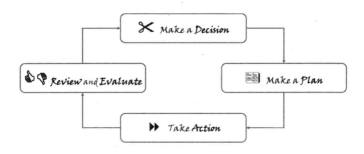

FIGURE 16: ACTION CYCLE

Having made a plan and taken action, Figure 16 reminds us that you must continually review and evaluate the results of your actions. You must also be prepared to review your decision and make a new plan. To do otherwise is to fall for the planning fallacy and have misplaced faith in a plan despite empirical evidence. The real world is always right, no matter how elegant your theory.

Right and Wrong

The concepts of right and wrong as absolutes are at their most straightforward in the arenas of mathematics and natural science, where logical proof and empirical evidence are possible. These are thus more domains for knowledge rather than wisdom.

Wisdom becomes necessary as the possibilities of absolute right and wrong, and of the comfortable certainties of unambiguous evidence, evaporate. Philosophers have argued for centuries about the possibility of moral absolutes. At two ends of the spectrum are:

- **Moral Absolutism**, which argues that some actions can be absolutely right or wrong regardless of the circumstances.
- **Moral Particularism**, which argues that actions can only be evaluated in the context of their particular circumstances.

Moral relativism is a form of moral particularism which suggests that the morality of actions must be assessed within the context of social or cultural norms.

As always, some synthesis is necessary. While we may never find a *"moral absolute"* on which all can agree, in any society there are clearly some moral values for which only the most extreme circumstances will provide an exception. As you move from smart to wise, you will become more adept at discerning the factors that lead you away from or towards society's norms, in any given situation.

Sixth Pillar:
FAIRNESS

FAIRNESS AS A CHOICE

In the moral sphere, good judgement is not enough. Wisdom must also include an understanding of when it is necessary to act upon your judgement, and the determination to do so. You must also be willing to take responsibility for your actions. Fairness arises from action – it requires the courage to choose what is right.

It is not a coincidence that the word fair means both honest or even-handed, and also pleasant and beautiful. Like judgement, fairness is often a fine balance. If you tilt the scales just a tiny amount, you reach one of the infinite varieties of unfairness. As soon as you act upon your judgement, you will start to change the situation and shift the balance point. This means that, in the real world, fairness may not always be an achievable ideal. Your wisdom will be measured by how you strive for it.

RIGHT ACTION

Right action is associated with wisdom because sometimes it is difficult or uncomfortable. It is the wise, not the easy or smart, choice.

Confidence and Responsibility

We rarely regret the mistakes we make as much as we regret the things we have not done. Right action is not about always making the "right" choice – you will make mistakes. It is about having the courage to act on the choice you believe is right and take responsibility for that choice. Wisdom speaks consistently on this matter:

> *"All you have to do in your life is go for broke. People might actually discuss whether you made a difference at all, but you, as that grain of sand, have done what you were called to do…"*
>
> **Bernice Johnson Reagon**

Making the choices that are true to you is what we have termed *authenticity*. The confidence to be authentic and be able to take responsibility for your choices comes from independence. You must cultivate some level of detachment from constraints that would prevent you from acting according to your conscience.

Speaking Truth to Power

We do not all have the power to act as we would wish. What you do have is the ability to tell others how you see the world. Good judgement means nothing if you fail to be honest with people. This can require real steel when the person you need to address has more authority and more power than you.

Honesty is simple, but it is not always easy. Among the hardest things you may have to do are those conversations that relay uncomfortable truths. It is not just because you don't like the discomfort or because you cherish your popularity: there is a real risk that, if it goes badly, the conversation can derail what you are trying to achieve.

Giving people bad, uncomfortable or unwanted news can flip their focus from rational to irrational, and their response can become unpredictable. This can quickly dominate and, if they have sufficient power, can hijack a whole agenda. It is no wonder, therefore, that we would often prefer simply to send an email. It's quick, it's detached and we can think it through and write it as we want to: no chance of mis-speaking. Of course, you know that this is the wrong approach.

The origins of the phrase *"speak truth to power"* lie in an injunction to Quakers in the eighteenth century, and the phrase was used explicitly in a polemical pamphlet in the 1950s. It has since been frequently reused. But the concept is, of course, far older: in ancient Greece, the concept of saying everything, being bold and speaking without fear was called *"parrhesia"*.

The challenge is how to do this effectively. Even if you discount the personal risks of losing face, being shouted at or facing sanctions, speaking fearlessly can change everything. So ensure that the change, if it comes, is controlled.

Fearless speaking is not about being brave enough to dive in: the courage you need is to face up to the complexity of your message and make the time to prepare. This unfortunately means living with the stress for a little longer. In planning, you have three objectives: communicate your message, control your emotional state and manage that of the other person. The common mistake is to treat the first of these as most or all of the challenge.

The key to controlling your emotions is preparation. Managing the other person's emotions is far harder. Often, there is nothing you can do. Four things that will help are:

1. Keep facts simple and express things as clearly and as succinctly as you can. Then stop speaking.

2. Give them time to work things out for themselves and listen carefully to their responses.

3. Give them a back door – when they get the message and need to save face, have some extra information to offer. That way, they can place the blame on not knowing that one fact, rather than hold out to avoid losing face.

4. Be prepared to declare that the situation has broken down and handle it appropriately. We will take a look at breakdowns and conflict soon.

EQUITY

Fairness is ultimately based on a respect for the differences between us. Yet these differences are the essence of humanity. It is difference that makes fairness difficult.

Adams and Equity

The industrial psychologist John Stacy Adams took a particular interest in fairness in the workplace. Starting from the work of social psychologists on how relationships are based on an evaluation of advantage and disadvantage, Adams investigated our perceptions of fairness. His theory, the *"Equity Theory"*, suggests that we make mental comparisons between ourselves and the people around us.

You do this by considering the ratio between perceived outcomes (the rewards you get) and perceived work (the effort you put in): O/W. If you perceive that the ratio for me and for you is equal, all feels fair. If you perceive that my ratio, O'/W', exceeds yours, the inequity will be demotivating. Likewise, you will also feel unfairly rewarded if O/W exceeds O'/W'.

Adams has effectively explained why people can be well-rewarded in absolute terms but be demotivated by an over-paid or low-productivity colleague. This can drive a number of behaviours which subconsciously tend to restore equity. Although some of us are more or less sensitive to inequity, it seems that our sense of equity is innate.

Equity and Diversity

> *"There is nothing more unequal than the equal treatment of unequal people."*
> **(This quote is often attributed to Thomas Jefferson.
> However, there is no source and the attribution is
> disputed by the Thomas Jefferson Foundation.)**

What this quote means is that if you treat everybody in the same way, then you will treat nobody fairly. Equity comes through treating each person in the way that is best calculated to serve their needs, meet their wants and bring out the best in them. This is the basis of entire theories of management and leadership, and wisdom lies in the ability to discern how best to treat each person to achieve fairness.

To be fair to any person, you need to understand what makes them different, to respect that distinctness and to harness it. The rewards are immense, however. It is the diversity of the people around you that can create the most subtle analysis, most potent problem-solving and most reliable decision-making.

Perception of Risk, Choices to Act, and Emotional Proximity

A risk is an uncertainty that can affect outcomes. Risks can be characterised by the impact should they occur and the likelihood that they will manifest. However, our subjective perception of risk is biased by many factors and one of the most important is emotional proximity – we worry more about threats that feel close to home than those that threaten strangers with whom we feel no connection. This informs a lot of policy making: it is smart politics, but poor wisdom.

When one charismatic and popular figure dies within our culture – Steve Jobs, for example – millions mourn their loss. Yet when millions die in a far part of the world, few shed a tear. Marketers and advertisers know the power of the specific to move us, and so will talk about the plight or the joy of one mother and child rather than of thousands of families. If you are wise, you can discern the true impact and meaning of events, be they very parochial or far away.

CONFLICT

Conflict arises from difference and can be very productive, harnessing diverse ideas and perspectives. However, it frequently gets out of control. Acquiring wisdom necessitates some expertise in handling conflict in a constructive way.

Your Own Conflict

Anger is not wise: it serves no purpose. Instead, it will distort your judgement and result in unfair treatment of the people around you. (Feigned anger as a tactic may, however, serve a purpose, as long as you remain in emotional control, but it is manipulative and therefore conflicts with your desire to maintain authenticity and integrity.) There is some evidence to suggest that we become better at controlling our temper as we age, but there will always be times when you struggle to master your emotions.

Not all conflict involves anger, but controlling your emotions is a necessary precursor to resolving conflict. It allows you to think clearly, understand the other person's point of view and follow a process towards resolution.

Breakdown Process

When a relationship has broken down, it's time to follow a process to rebuild it.

1. Declare that the breakdown has occurred.
   "At our last meeting, things went wrong."

2. State the outcomes you want to work towards.
   "What I would like to achieve is…"

3. Ask for the other person's outcome.
   "What would you like us to achieve?"

4. Share the facts, being honest about your own shortcomings. Be prepared to acknowledge different interpretations of events and take care to distinguish facts from opinions.
   "What happened at our last meeting was…"

5. State your commitments. This may include a recap of what you have been committed to in the past, but must focus on what you are committed to now.
   "I am committed to…"

6. Invite their commitments, but be prepared for them to decline to make any at this stage.
   "What are you committed to, now?"

7. Look for what is missing: in the data, in the process, in your different perceptions of what is possible.
   "What was missing for me was a feeling that I had all of the information and feedback that I needed."

8. Look for options: alternative ways to mend the breakdown.
   "Here are some possible ways forward for us… What ways can you suggest?"

9. Put together a plan – actions, requests, promises.
   "This is what I propose to do… and this is what I would need from you."

10. Reiterate your commitment.
    "I think this plan is a good one, and I am committed to pursuing it as best I can."

Other People's Conflict

Bringing harmony to conflict, through mediating or arbitrating, requires wisdom. It is also an excellent way of exercising and developing your wisdom, and of gauging your progress: people will only ask you to get involved when they have respect for your wisdom.

Mediation

An impartial person helps two or more others to reach an acceptable resolution.

Arbitration

An impartial person provides an external resolution to a dispute.

Mediating and arbitrating are, however, just processes which can be learnt and applied. Arbitration requires an in-depth understanding of the circumstances and the wisdom to find the right solution. Mediation requires the patience and wisdom to allow two parties to find their own solution, and the mutual respect between disputants and mediator that will allow the agreement to stick.

Whether mediating or arbitrating, the need for fairness imposes constraints on the way you should act.

1. Build in time for rapport-building. Agreements are more easily made between people who know and like one another. It is easy to sustain a conflict when we perceive the other as sharing nothing with us or, worse still, as some impersonal "other". Find some common concerns or enthusiasms to build rapport.

2.   Get everybody's feelings, perceptions and positions out in the open and seek for each party to acknowledge the perspectives of the others.

3.   Ask questions and listen carefully. Clarify, re-state and translate into terms that the other parties can understand.

4.   Separate facts from interpretations and feelings. Find ways to validate or disprove the evidence that each party presents, so that you can all work from a consistent set of verified facts.

5.   Look for a small piece of common ground from which to start to form agreement. It is easier to move from a small agreement to a bigger one, than from disagreement to an agreement.

6.   Avoid any form of threat or any criticism of the parties – particularly impugning their integrity or ascribing motivations to their actions. Do not allow personal attacks.

7.   Keep negotiations on track and do not let significant issues be avoided. You may choose to postpone a topic to stick to a sequence you believe more productive, but explicitly track all of the issues.

MORAL PURPOSE

Difficult decisions are the domain of wisdom. At some stage you will bump into major ethical questions – few have challenged humanity more than *"do the ends justify the means?"* To what extent is it fair or wise to countenance unfair acts in order to achieve a fair outcome?

Moral Virtue

Aristotle did not believe we could pre-define what is right or wrong in any situation. Instead, he argued that virtue reflects an ability to perceive what is right in any situation, and act accordingly. Moral virtue is the desire to act fairly, so that your motivation is an essential component.

Personal Values

We often build our ethical basis on the foundation of our personal values. Your values define the "musts", "shoulds" and "oughts" in your life. They are underlying feelings or assumptions that drive the decisions you make, or give you your sense of the decision you would like to make. They set out what in life – or any particular context – is most important to you.

The problem is that we mostly acquire our values as we are growing up: from our families, our friends, our schooling, our society, religion and the media. Very few of us take time to re-examine our values as mature adults.

Develop Your Values

A part of your path to wisdom is reflection and introspection – this is an especially worthy subject. Take each part of your life (your well-being, family, home, career, finances, friends, hobbies, job, learning, spiritual life or philosophy) and examine it carefully. What are your values now? What drives the decisions you make and feels most important to you?

Now review objectively where you acquired those values and whether they feel truly authentic to you now. If they do not, what values would replace them? They may be radically new values or subtle re-interpretations. As you complete each area of your life, re-visit the areas you have already done and check for consistency: conflicting values can lead to emotional stress.

The Cynic Tradition

While this group of Greek philosophers, which emerged in the fourth century BCE just after the death of Socrates, gave us the word "cynic", they were by no means cynical in the modern sense. Quite the opposite: they believed that the only distinctions that really mattered were ones of true and false values. All of the social conventions such as dress, etiquette and ownership were artificial and worthless.

As a result Diogenes, the leading Cynic, dressed in rags and lived off scraps, earning himself the nickname Kynikos, "like a dog". He also rejected nationality as another arbitrary convention, declaring himself a citizen of the world, or "cosmopolitan".

Unity of Virtues: Morality and Intellect

The Greeks distinguished moral from intellectual virtues. Moral virtues embody right conduct, fair choices and wise actions, while intellectual virtues are about valuing truth for its own sake, scepticism and the courage to defend and act upon your reasoning.

Plato and Aristotle believed in *"the unity of the virtues"*, meaning that to have one virtue was to have them all – that to be virtuous meant having all virtues. So, for example, to be tolerant of diversity, we must be so for good reasons rather than simply for personal gain. If we acted that way just for our own benefit, then the tolerance would not be a virtue. Can an academic seeking the truth really be virtuous, if the state successfully coerces them into not publishing their findings?

On the other hand, it is possible to envisage another academic pursuing the truth relentlessly and publishing it under threat to their liberty, yet at the same time treating their research staff with contempt and abuse. Human beings and our motivations are complex: people and institutions are rarely "good" or "bad".

Once again, wisdom requires that we evaluate the whole, but are careful to avoid simplistic judgements.

AUTHORITY

THE AUTHORITY OF WISDOM

Wisdom has a special kind of authority, which can be encapsulated in the phrase:

"Say less: achieve more"

The chart on the following page shows how smart people can become either boring or influential through communicating more and more.

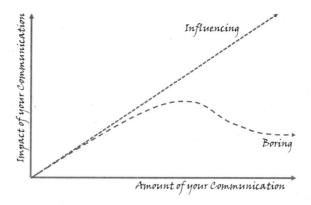

FIGURE 17: THE IMPACT OF COMMUNICATION

Initially, as your wisdom increases, you need to say only a little more to achieve a far greater influence. However, something paradoxical comes with wisdom: as you say less, you become more influential. People listen more carefully and are more minded to act on their interpretation of what you say – even if what you say offers less true direction as to how to act.

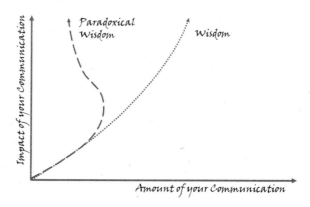

FIGURE 18: THE IMPACT OF WISE COMMUNICATION

COMMUNICATION

Communication is coded into human DNA. We cannot do other than communicate.

As you move from smart to wise, you will be honing your communication skills on two levels – the communication you *"leak into the world"* through your very presence, and the skilled communication that you use artfully to gain influence over others.

Leaked Communication

"You cannot do other than communicate" means that we leak information about ourselves that others will interpret. So building your authority and perceived influence must involve constantly fashioning the information you communicate unconsciously. This will allow you to control the first impressions that you make on other people.

Charisma

Some will refer to this leaked communication as your charisma, although the term is most usually used to refer to the positive impact you make on people. You will want to make a captivating first impression that is both positive and sustainable. This will give you the ability to inspire and influence others.

We do not act as a result of the world around us, but as a result of the way we represent it in our minds, in terms of our mental models, emotions and physiological responses. Therefore, to affect others, you need to affect the way they perceive you and the emotions that they attach to your presence.

Develop Charisma

Charisma is learnable. By adjusting how you behave, you will change the way people around you perceive you.

Posture

Keep a relaxed, upright, and open body posture. Keep your hands away from your face and keep your stance and movements broadly symmetric. Lean slightly towards the people you are speaking with.

Gesture

Keep your gestures natural, matching the sense of what you are saying. Avoid touching other parts of your body as you are speaking and keep your hands loose with palms open. Allowing yourself to move fluidly portrays confidence and enthusiasm. Nod, smile and show understanding when other people are speaking. Keep your gestures calm and unrushed.

Expression

Smiling is magical – it portrays confidence and invites others to smile back, which will make them feel good. Look at the people you are speaking with, catching their eye – whether an individual or a large group – and maintain eye contact when speaking with small groups or one-to-one.

Impression

Use your choice of clothes and your grooming to emphasise the impression that you want to make. In Polonius' advice to Laertes (William Shakespeare, *Hamlet*), he says "*the apparel oft proclaims the man*".

Listening

Ask questions to encourage people to speak and listen carefully, using nods and smiles to show you are paying attention and value what you are hearing. Develop their points with insights or simply agree, rather than repeating their point – which suggests you want them to like you.

Valuing

Demonstrate that you value people by remembering their names (80% of that talent is caring enough in the first place). When you are speaking to a group, hold eye contact with each individual to make them feel you are speaking personally to them.

Slow

Do not be rushed. Take a few deep breaths to calm and relax you before speaking. Your voice will now fall to the lower end of your vocal register and you will feel more in control. Use pauses to further emphasise the importance and measured nature of what you are saying.

What you say

Make your message interesting by avoiding conventional *"isn't it awful"* or *"don't we all know it"* topics. Instead offer insight, controversial ideas or counter-intuitive interpretations. Look for ways to explain complex ideas simply and to introduce new, innovative thinking.

How you say it

Be precise and concise in your language. Practice stopping when you have made your point and get comfortable with silence. Use relevant examples and analogies to bring ideas to life. Vary your pace, using up-tempo rhythms to convey enthusiasm, and slow down to convey importance. Lower the volume to draw people in and use pauses to build tension.

Authenticity

Authenticity is a theme running through *Smart to Wise*, and is important in establishing your authority. Where the information you leak is consistent with your deliberate communication, the two will act to support one another and increase your authority. Where, however, the messages are incongruent – if, for example, you say something clearly and precisely, yet your body language betrays a lack of confidence – that incongruence will undermine your authority.

Skilled Communication

Skilled communication is your ability to convey the essential nature of a situation in a way that makes it easy for others to comprehend. It involves simplifying where appropriate, but knowing when to retain the complexity that is essential for understanding. Skilled communicators can structure an argument, create a narrative arc, use analogy, metaphor and allegory and select compelling examples.

Skilled communicators also know that a rational argument will not always persuade, no matter how compelling the logic. So you must learn how to appeal to empathy as well as understanding, and how to read the non-verbal cues that hold the key to our emotional state. Influencing others is about creating a shared experience.

Influence can be dangerous though. If your opinions carry too much influence, then you will inhibit independent thinking in the people around you. Deference can be dangerous, not just because you may be wrong. You may be right, but there may be other even better ideas available. So use your influence to encourage better thinking.

Less is more

When you say less, you allow others to fill the gaps. Not only does this bring out their insights; it often leaves them thinking that you were a step ahead of them! Children's author Dick Bruna says:

> *"If you put very few things on a page, you leave lots of room for the imagination."*

Go one step further: cultivate silence. When you become comfortable with silence, you will start to notice magic happen. Leave silence at the end of sentences, before sentences; even in the middle of sentences. People often fill it for you. In the silence is the truth.

PERSUASION

At some stage you will want to persuade others to your point of view, secure agreement to act or enlist their support. The skills of persuasion often seem magical, yet they can be learnt like any other skill.

Presence of Mind

Great persuaders never rush. They always take time to compose themselves and to marshal their argument before putting it.

> *"Speak when you are angry and you will make the best speech you will ever regret."*

Ambrose Bierce

The ability to speak persuasively when you are under pressure requires great presence of mind. Happily, there are techniques that you can practice to calm you and give you time to respond resourcefully.

Develop Presence of Mind

Mental Preparation

Use the SCOPE process to take a mental timeout: Stop, Clarify the situation, and what outcomes you want from it, Organise your thoughts before you Proceed. Be ready to Evaluate your progress constantly, and Stop again if you need to. During your preparation, look at the situation from different points of view; not just your own, but from other people's perspectives.

Physical Preparation

Deliberately adopt a confident posture, square on to the person or people you are addressing, and slow your breathing by taking deeper breaths. These physiological changes will send signals to your brain, starting to calm down the release of stress hormones.

Reacting

Ask for clarification to ensure you have all of the facts and also to give you thinking time. If you are asked a question, you can also repeat it back to confirm. Use the same key words to show the other person that you really understand them. Harness the power of silence to think and to create a heightened sense of expectation. A response after a silence always sounds more considered and persuasive.

Controlling

There is no harm in asking for time to think. The message you are giving is "*this is important; I am taking it seriously*". You can then ask more questions to give you further insights or spark ideas. If necessary, suggest returning to the issue at a later time – suggest a specific next step.

Responding

There are many formulas for structured responses that will make you sound authoritative, by being concise and well structured. Try PREC or PPP:

PREC

- state your **Point**
- give your **Reasons**
- cite an **Example** or analogy, then
- make a Call to **Action**

PPP

- establish the situation, or **Position**
- describe the **Pressures** that make this important
- state your recommendation, decision or **Point of View**

Rhetoric

Once, any good education would include the art of rhetoric – the techniques for using speech or writing to persuade. It is never too late to study the way great persuasive speeches can be constructed using patterns of language. Rhetoriticians use their words to manipulate not just ideas, but also emotions. The central concepts of Greek rhetoric were appeals to:

Logos: reason, logic and analysis
Ethos: ethics, integrity, conduct, values and character
Pathos: emotion, care, concern, sympathy and empathy

One of the best ways to study rhetoric is to read or listen to great speeches. When you read or hear a phrase that resonates, stop and consider how it is constructed and what it evokes in you, the listener. This will be a far more pleasant way to understand the figures of speech than studying techniques with dry Latin and Greek names like *epitrope, aposiopesis, litotes* or *synecdoche.*

The Sophist Tradition

Of all the movements in philosophy, few have drawn more criticism than the Sophists, Greek teachers and philosophers in the times before Socrates revolutionised philosophy. They taught Greek nobles how to argue and put the best possible case for their argument – regardless of their own convictions. We still use the word "sophistry" to denote clever, though logically-flawed, arguments. Ironically, the Greek word "sophist" meant "wise man" – from "sophia", and hence the word "sophisticated".

Rhetoric was seen as a fundamental skill for playing a full part in society. One leading Sophist, Isocrates, wrote:

"I do think that the study of political discourse can help more than any other thing to stimulate and form such qualities of character."

The Sophists taught five components of their rhetorical art: invention, arrangement, style, memory and delivery. Arguably they were way ahead of their time, because they taught that excellence is neither a product of fate nor a prerogative of a noble birth. Instead it is a learnable skill (or *"techne"*). Sophists challenged both the social order of the day and the ascendancy of the gods in deciding our fate.

Far from being derided in their time, the great Sophist teachers and orators such as Isocrates, Gorgias and Protagoras, were highly respected and highly paid professionals who had studied and mastered an important art. The paucity of great – or even good – oratory in modern public life would make them weep.

INSPIRATION

Smart people have ideas that we take up because they are smart: they solve a problem neatly, they offer an attractive way forward, or they represent an accurate diagnosis. The ideas that come from wisdom do all of that, but they can also take us further. We feel like we are seeing something from a new perspective or something completely new that no one else could have seen. The ideas move or excite us. Wisdom inspires us to hope that we too can do better.

The Visionary

To see further, you must look beneath the surface of things to perceive new possibilities. This can allow you to find ways to accomplish what others may think are impossible. We covered learning to perceive deeply as the Second Pillar. It requires expertise and an accumulation of experience, coupled with the skill of probing for and noticing the tiny details that matter, but are intelligible only to the prepared mind.

Visionaries often become so only after much hard work and immersion. This gives their ideas intellectual integrity, which we readily perceive and deeply respect. We want to follow a visionary for the excitement of a quest.

The Enchanter

How you present your vision also matters. Have you noticed that visionaries often use symbols and dramatic language and imagery to communicate? Naming and representing things with iconic images is an important skill in communicating passion and excitement.

"People are the size you make them feel."

Vanessa Branson

When you can give people a feeling that your ideas can transform their lives with their power or beauty, they will willingly follow you. You can do this when you:

1. Fold your idea into a powerful narrative that enhances our sense of who we are
2. Link your idea to a real sense of purpose and meaning
3. Create simple iconic representations of your idea, with a name or an image
4. Highlight the elegance and beauty in your idea

5. Give people a sense that they can attain deeper understanding or a greater level of skill

POLITICAL WISDOM

The most successful people are often not those with the greatest intellect but those who can get along better with the widest range of people. Political wisdom is knowing how to sense people's moods, handle them effectively to get the best from them and to respond appropriately to people in a range of circumstances. With this, you can achieve practical objectives by bringing people together, aligning opinions and inciting them to make change.

This is essentially what politics is about. Do not for one minute think that politics begins or ends in a legislative chamber or among legislators. Wherever two people come together, there is politics. You need to be able to harness the experience, knowledge and skills of the people around you to transform the world.

Political Animals: Are you an Owl, a Fox, a Donkey or a Sheep?

Simon Baddeley and Kim James developed a useful model of political behaviour that works equally well in a range of contexts from local to national politics and from social to workplace settings. It considers that our political awareness can be high or low and that we can act with integrity or engage in psychological game-playing.

This allowed them to identify four iconic behaviours that they describe as "clever" – or "smart" in our language – "wise", "inept" and "innocent". They allocated iconic animals to each of these states.

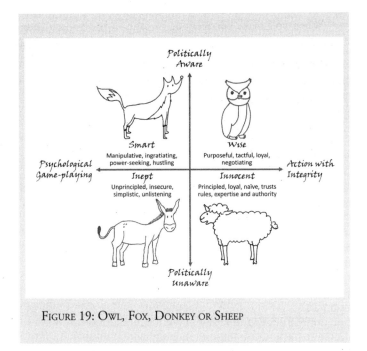

FIGURE 19: OWL, FOX, DONKEY OR SHEEP

Connecting with People

"Networking" is a subject that causes more fear in business people than any other. But this ugly word hides a beautifully simple concept – networking is nothing more than getting to know more people.

Take the opportunities that are available to you to meet new people, and then take an interest in them. This is nothing more than taking an interest in the world, and accessing the resources of the people you meet, to contribute to your knowledge and thinking. Build your influence and credibility by listening for ways you can help them, and by being generous with your own ideas and experience.

When you make connections to other people, those people will slowly grow in wisdom, and you will grow with them. Nowadays you can make use of appropriate web-based social media tools to help you, and their importance currently shows every sign of increasing over the coming years.

Mastermind Groups

There is a saying that *"you are as wise as your network of contacts"*. This is true, if you can harness their wisdom. One powerful way to do this is to list, from among your contacts, a diverse group of three or four who you consider to be the most wise, challenging, insightful and stimulating thinkers. Meet up with these people as a group from time to time and talk about what concerns each of you, what changes or trends you are observing, and what they might mean.

Influencing People

The psychology of influence has received a lot of attention recently in popular books (my own included) and magazines. It may still feel as if some people have it and others don't, but the techniques can all be learnt. The mistake that many smart people make is to think that with these techniques, they can manipulate anyone to do anything. When the techniques fail, they fear that they will never learn them properly.

The truth is plain. No one can be sure of influencing you: you have your own mind. All that anyone can do is use effective means to make you more likely to do what they want, or to agree with their conclusions.

Influencing means creating a strong case and presenting

it well; making me more likely to pay attention to you and to evaluate your ideas objectively. We will leave the wizardry to illusionists and stage hypnotists, and examine some simple lessons from psychology.

Charisma
We talked about charisma earlier in this chapter and, without a doubt, if you cultivate charisma and a confident presence, people will be more likely to accept your ideas.

Fairness
We also talked about fairness and equity as the sixth pillar. If I have done something for you, then you will feel a certain measure of obligation to reciprocate. Look after the people that you are connected to, and this will foster a loyalty that will lead them to support you when you need it.

Group Judgements
The fifth pillar is about judgement, but often we have too many decisions to make and not enough time to exercise our judgement. We are content, when what is at stake is not too great, to follow the judgements of people around us. If you can show me that you have persuaded enough people, I may not need persuading. This requires that I perceive the people you have persuaded as being sufficiently like me to share my interests in the situation.

Your Judgement
I may also be inclined to accept your judgement with little questioning or doubt, if you can persuade me that you have sufficient expertise, skill, experience and credibility in this domain. Fundamentally, authority itself is influential.

Authenticity

If you can show me how a decision or an action is consistent with who I perceive myself to be, it will be easier to decide, or act, in the way you suggest. If you can show me that to not act, or to take another decision is not consistent with my self-image, then that perceived inauthenticity will work strongly in your favour.

Perception

Being able to perceive the consequences of our actions helps us to decide. Show the opportunities and the threats of the ideas you are advocating. The biggest motivators, and therefore the most powerful weapons of influence, are self-interest and fear.

Evolution

One motivator is often forgotten, but arguably, it defines our species – curiosity. You can often influence people to try some course of action for no other reason than for the sheer pleasure of learning something new. It has driven humanity to exploration, scientific investigation and discovery of vast new opportunities. As long as you offer a fair assessment of the risks involved, you need not fear for the integrity of inducing me to act on curiosity.

Valuing People

There is a simple mindset that will guide you to connecting deeply with the people you meet. It will leave them open to influence and persuasion, feeling that you are a particularly charismatic and inspiring person.

Value everyone you meet. Treat them as though you are the only person who knows their secret: that they are really incredibly rich, powerful, intelligent and wise. When you make people feel that special, sincerely, they cannot not feel a little in your debt.

The Wisdom of Authority

There is an irony at the heart of authority: the more of it you gain, the more you risk abandoning wisdom. People defer to authority (hierarchical and intellectual) for all sorts of reasons, not just for perceived wisdom. This is dangerous because even if you are wise, you do not have a monopoly on wisdom. If you are wise, you know you may be wrong and that trust in you, at the level of faith, is foolishness.

Do not risk losing the valuable insights, ideas and analysis that other people can offer. Make it as easy as possible for them to give you their opinions, and to challenge yours. Don't try to defend your ideas, nor react against the challenge, but assess it with care and reward people for their willingness to contribute. Ask them questions and listen to their ideas, and avoid falling into the *"anchoring trap"*.

The anchoring trap is our pre-disposition to take the first thing we hear as the fixed point against which to measure every contribution. This, especially when it comes from a voice of authority, can frame a whole debate, limiting our appreciation of other points of view. The anchoring trap confers an advantage to the first speaker, but is dangerous when the first speaker is wrong. If you invite contributions before you speak, you avoid biasing other people, and have the opportunity to assess everyone's ideas before you make up your mind.

Conclusion

Wisdom leads you away from the expectation that the world is a conveniently simple and orderly place. Wisdom too is not a neat and tidy concept. This means that there are loose ends to address – even if we cannot tie them all up.

TOWARDS A UNIFYING PICTURE OF WISDOM

Our seven pillars do not stand alone. We have already illustrated, in figure 14, that the first four lead towards the idea of character, and create a platform to support the second three.

We can now show how these concepts work together to create a powerful presence in the world.

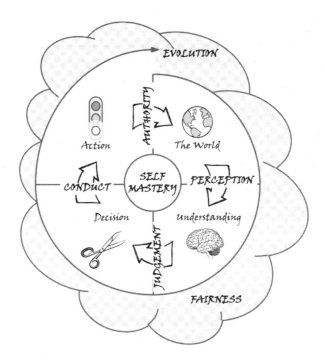

FIGURE 20: A UNIFYING PICTURE OF WISDOM

In figure 20, let us start with the world.

Perception
It is your perception that links the world to your mind. With your perception, you create understanding of what is happening around you.

Judgement
You apply your judgement to that understanding to make decisions about what is right for you to advocate or do.

Conduct

It is through conduct that you translate your decisions into action and manage your relationships with others.

Authority

Your actions are the way you will influence the world, and having the authority to influence people allows you to create change.

Evolution

When you have been around this cycle, something changes. If you are capable of learning from this, then you too will change: you will evolve. The cycle continues.

Fairness

Surrounding all of your interaction with the world are the choices you make, the values that drive you and the extent to which you take responsibility for your perceptions, judgements and conduct, and for the influence you have on the world.

Self-Mastery

At the core of all of this is self-mastery – your ability to know and control yourself, your emotions and your behaviours. This is the strength you have to drive the cycle and, as a result of all of it, who you are.

FUZZY WISDOM

When we considered Moral Purpose at the sixth pillar, we talked about the unity of virtues and the Greek idea that to have one virtue was to have all. Virtue as an "all or nothing" concept seemed an unsatisfactory model.

So we come to the question of the "unity of wisdom". Must every pillar be strong before the world will call you "wise"? Or can you be wise in one area and remain merely smart – or even foolish – in other domains and areas?

Is wisdom all or nothing: is lacking judgement, or fairness, or self-mastery, enough to render you "not wise"? Do you need the whole package to attain wisdom? This seems unreasonable. Many of the people we observe and regard as wise have shortcomings.

So is it enough to master one aspect of wisdom for people to see you as wise, perhaps great judgement, right conduct or deep perception? This seems too limited a criterion for wisdom. It is almost as if too much foolishness or smartness will overpower a sense of wisdom. We need a different way of looking at wisdom.

Adulthood

Let's take a more familiar concept to help us understand. When does a child become an adult? Is it at 16 or at 18, or maybe at 13, or 15? Even within one culture, there are different measures. At time of writing, in the UK, we must stay at school until 16, with legislation to raise it to 18, and some Government advisers advocating that we reduce it back to 14, as it was in the 1940s. We can buy alcohol and cigarettes at 18 too – up from 16 for cigarettes a few years ago. We can marry at 16, but need parental consent until 18. We can join the armed forces at 16 (or 18 as an officer trainee) but cannot serve in a fighting capacity until 18. We can join the Police at 18, become a PCSO (Police Community Support Officer) at 16 and join the fire service at 18.

Across the world, where there is compulsory schooling, the ages of leaving school range from 10 to 18, and the age of sexual consent varies from 12 to 20 (with a few special cases) and the age of homosexual consent (where it is legal) ranges from 13 to 21. Various world religions and cultures recognise different ages for the transition to adulthood – or "coming of age". In Theravada Buddhism it is 20, while in Shinto it starts at 11 for boys and 12 for girls. Where the purchase of alcohol is legal, the age limit varies from 16 to 21, and the age requirement for military service ranges from 15 to 21.

Figure 21 is a graphical answer to the question "what age is adulthood?".

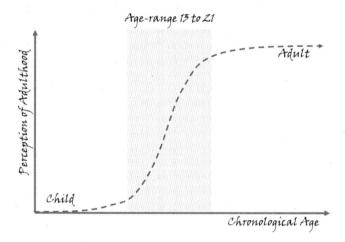

FIGURE 21: ADULTHOOD

When are we wise?

Figure 21 illustrates something known as *"fuzzy logic"*. Rather than more common "two-state" logic where something is either yes or no, on or off, in fuzzy logic there is an accumulation of factors. Below some level, a system has most of the characteristics of one status – and most people would adjudge it one way. Beyond another level of accumulated factors, most would now assess the system to be in the other state. So it is with wisdom. If you have enough characteristics, then most will judge you to be wise, and if you have too few, many will not see you as wise at all. In the middle, as you accumulate more elements of wisdom, you will approach what we may loosely call "true wisdom".

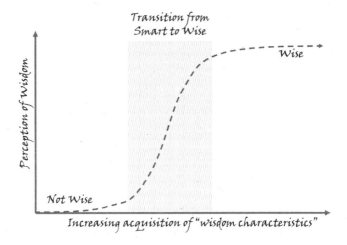

FIGURE 22: WISDOM

A NEVER-ENDING JOURNEY

If Figure 22 tells us anything it is this: wisdom is a subtle concept which develops slowly and then grows rapidly, one element building upon another, until it is largely in place. And then it keeps on growing. Your journey to wisdom will never end. There will never be a time when all will call you wise. But maybe, someday soon perhaps, you will first perceive that someone does. Allow yourself an inward smile. And keep going.

Continue your journey at www.smarttowise.co.uk.

About the Author

Mike Clayton has been searching for wisdom all of his life. He is fascinated by all branches of knowledge, from management theory to theoretical physics, from linguistics to psychology, and from history to philosophy. Learning is more than an objective; it's a life-long mission.

Mike comes from a family that valued education for its own sake, as well as the opportunities it can create, and he did pretty well at school and at university, gaining a PhD in the physics of quantum phenomena at the lowest temperatures. He then left university and a possible academic career for business, starting his first career as a management consultant with Deloitte, specialising in the delivery of large complex projects. Since leaving university, Mike has continually hankered to return, to study again.

Mike's second career was as a management trainer and coach, specialising in developing project management and leadership skills. Mike's programmes showed participants how to use powerful self-management and communication techniques to help them to manage and lead the people around them. During this time, he founded two training businesses and trained many thousands of people.

Now in his third career, Mike is focusing his energies on writing and speaking, delivering his training mostly through large group seminars. *Smart to Wise* is Mike's eighth book, and his second with Marshall Cavendish.

Mike lives in Hampshire, England, with his family.

To book Mike as a consultant or speaker for your event, you can contact him through his personal website, at www.mikeclayton.co.uk, or via the Smart to Wise website: www.smarttowise.co.uk.

ALSO BY MIKE CLAYTON

Risk Happens! Managing risk and avoiding failure in business projects, **Marshall Cavendish Business**

The Yes-No Book, **Prentice Hall**

Brilliant Project Leader, **Prentice Hall**

Brilliant Stress Management, **Prentice Hall**

Brilliant Time Management, **Prentice Hall**

Brilliant Influence, **Prentice Hall**

The Handling Resistance Pocketbook, **Management Pocketbooks**

The Management Models Pocketbook, **Management Pocketbooks**